Camping With Kids

How to Plan a Trip the Whole Family Will Enjoy

Camping With Kids

How to Plan a Trip the Whole Family Will Enjoy

BY DON AND PAM WRIGHT

Copyright 1992 by Cottage Publications, Inc.

Printed in the United States of America

Camping With Kids

ISBN 0-937877-09-3 $9.95

Cottage Publications, Inc.
24396 Pleasant View Dr., Elkhart, IN 46517 (219/875-8618)

Distributed by The Career Press
180 Fifth Avenue
P.O. Box 34
Hawthorne, NJ 07507 (1-800-CAREER-1)

Contents

Dedication

To those four wonderful, loving people who were always ready and willing to go camping with us: our children -- Chris, Thad, Micah and Sarah.

Introduction

More than 20 years have passed since we started camping with kids. We had been active campers before that, but careers, college and the daily pressures of starting a family forced us to postpone most of our camping activities for a few years. We started going camping with our four kids in the 1970s because, quite frankly, camping was the most economical way for us to travel as a family.

It would have been great if we could have prepared for family camping by reading a book on the subject, but there was none. Trailer Life Magazine, which we read avidly long before we bought our first RV, published occasional articles on the subject, but those usually raised more questions than they answered.

In the end, we learned how to camp with kids by doing it.

And boy, did we learn!

By the mid-1970s, we were taking regular writing assignments from the magazines published by Trailer Life Enterprises, including livability tests of travel trailers, fifth-wheels, motorhomes, folding camping trailers, pickup campers and trailer-towing vehicles of all kinds. We were on the road virtually every opportunity Don could find away from his newspaper editor job in Kettering, Ohio. And of course, those trips involved camping with our kids.

All our weekends were spent camping. Every vacation was spent camping. Family conversations began focusing on meeting for a thorough discussion of the possibilities. We offer our suggestions and ask the kids for their ideas.

Our children seldom propose any long-distance trips. Instead, they almost always will state a preference for returning to destinations they visited on earlier trips. Frequently, we've discovered that we can include one or more of those destinations within the context of our vacation travel. However, we generally try to steer the overall trip planning toward either a destination we've never visited or one we have not visited for a few years. By varying our selections, we can broaden the children's travel experiences and not lock ourselves into reliving the same types of experiences trip after trip. One of the best ways to begin planning a family camping vacation is to attend a couple of local travel and vacation shows that are generally held in January, February or March in most sections of the country. Destination-type campgrounds and tourism agencies are present at those shows and will gladly provide a wealth of information about the places they represent.

It is possible for the family planning meeting to end without final decisions on either direction or destination simply because we are unable to reach consensus on where the vacation ought to be spent. That's no problem; it simply means that we need to do more research and gather additional information about the primary alternatives that are being considered.

A typical disagreement could follow this pattern: Don and one or two of the boys might want to combine camping and fishing in the northwoods of Minnesota or Canada while Pam and our daughter and another son prefer to tour the New England states. A compromise might be a trip to Maine that combines both sightseeing and fishing.

Even when a consensus is reached, additional research often is desirable, and that research should involve all members of the family. If we're going to Maine, where should we camp and how long should we stay there? Should we set up a base camp and take short day trips from there, or should we plan moves to specific destinations every day or every two days? Maybe we should not follow any schedule but instead, spend each night in a different place. What route should we travel from Indiana to Maine? Should we return on the same route or a different one? Do we want to take side trips? If so, which ones are most appealing and how much time should be devoted to them? While we're in Maine, how many days will be allotted to shopping and sightseeing, and where will those activities take place? How many days will we devote to fishing, and where will we do that?

Research assignments are given to family members:

•Since Thad thinks he'd like to stop at Hershey, Pennsylvania, on the way, he is asked to write to the Pennsylvania tourism department and the Hershey Chamber of Commerce for travel brochures.

•Because Micah wants to go fishing at Moosehead Lake in Maine, he is assigned the job of gathering pertinent information about fishing, boating and camping facilities at the lake. He also is expected to research nearby attractions and activities for family members who do not want to fish, writing to local tourism bureaus or chambers of commerce for information.

•Sarah is assigned to researching potential attractions to visit during one-day excursions along the Maine coast. She will write to various tourist agencies in Maine for literature.

•Chris is given the job of purchasing updated editions of campground directories and picking up appropriate tour books from the local auto club office. He also will spend some time looking through our favorite travel magazines for articles about off-the-beaten-track destinations and attractions.

  •Pam will assist Sarah and also investigate opportunity for a side trip to Boston -- an area of the country we've never yet visited as a family and one she very much wants to see.

  •Don will map the trip, taking into account the possible side trips and dividing the vacation into possible one-day segments ending at prospective campgrounds along the way.

  Each family member is expected to complete his or her assignment in time for another family meeting in one month. At that meeting, Thad offers his reasons why we ought to spend one day in Hershey, Pennsylvania. He tells about attractions in the area (focusing on Hershey's Chocolate World Visitor's Center) and provides information about prospective campgrounds. He points out that although visiting Hershey will require we take a longer route to Maine, the detour will allow us to visit the retail outlet shops of Reading as well as seeing the quaint village of Kutztown for the first time.

  After some discussion, the family votes not to visit Hershey because of the extra travel time required, but Thad is assigned to recommend an alternative side trip that is less time-consuming.

  Micah has thoroughly researched the Moosehead Lake area of Maine where he wants to go fishing. He points out there are several attractions in the area for family members who don't want to fish -- including visiting the Eveleth-Crafts-Sheridan Historical Home, a Victorian-style free museum in Greenville. He also recommends we set aside at least one day for touring part of the North Maine Woods wilderness area. His recommendations are accepted with the provision that a loose day-to-day schedule will be maintained while we're in that area.

Since the family has previously traveled through Maine, Sarah's job of researching coastal attractions is not difficult; she had decided beforehand to concentrate on areas such as Kennebunkport, Boothbay Harbor and Acadia National Park. She attracts the boys' attention by recommending a tour of the Fisheries Research Lab in Boothbay Harbor, and she suggests spending a full two days walking through Dock Square in Kennebunkport after gorging ourselves on seafood at the coastal lobster pounds. Her suggestions are supported unanimously.

Pam's side trip to Boston is scheduled as part of our return home over her objection that our family often changes its plans during the last leg of a camping trip. "I can see now that my chances of visiting Boston are not very good," she says. The other family members sympathize. Attractions we'll see -- if we make it to Boston -- include Arnold Arboretum, Bunker Hill, Boston Naval Historical Park and a walking tour of Beacon Hill.

Chris found a few off-the-beaten-path destinations but points out that our route to Maine will take us rather close to a major international attraction that none of us has ever seen -- Niagara Falls. Everyone agrees we should not miss this opportunity to see the falls, so agreement is reached to forego all other side trips if necessary in order to spend a couple of days there.

* * *

As with most of our family camping trips, we decide to maintain a casual schedule. We'll see Niagara Falls when we get there, and until then, we'll be free to travel at whatever speed seems appropriate at the time. Except for spending two or three days fishing Moosehead Lake and touring North Maine Woods, no specific amount of time will be allotted to any one locale. No campground reservations will be made because doing so will hold us to too tight a schedule.

There is more planning to be done before we'll be ready to leave for Maine, however. Generally, preparation can be divided into long-range and short-range planning, with short-range planning including preparations made just prior to departure and long-range planning including all other preparations.

Here are some examples of long-range planning:
- Deciding whether to take friends along
- Assigning duties and chores
- Estimating each child's expense needs
- Preparing clothing lists
- Doing an inventory of supplies and equipment
- Preparing equipment lists
- Preparing supplies lists
- Buying clothing, supplies and equipment

Short-range planning includes actually packing the camping vehicle, planning daily meals and deciding exactly when to hit the road.

After determining where to go on a camping trip, we try to consider whether one or more of the kids will be allowed to invite a friend along. We believe it is important to make this decision early in the trip-planning process because the presence of a guest or two can have a direct affect on the type and amount of supplies, equipment, food and clothing that are packed.

Frankly, we're a little surprised that more families do not include their children's friends on camping trips. The

most common reasons for not allowing kids to invite
friends are a lack of space, a lack of money or an un-
willingness to take responsibility for the friends. We cannot
argue about the responsibility issue; that is something
dictated largely by individual family philosophy. We have
decided against taking our kids' friends along on trips
several times simply because we wanted our vacation to be
free of concern for the welfare of non-family members, or
because not having a non-family member along gave us the
freedom of spending extra time with each of our children
without worrying about how the friend would keep busy. In
addition, it has been our experience that friends should not
travel with another family for longer than a week's vacation. When the trip is longer than that, even good friends
can get tired of each other.

ALWAYS ROOM FOR ONE MORE

But as for a lack of space or money, we've never
regarded those aspects as being very important. Camping
with five or six kids is no more difficult than doing it with
four, and the increased cost is negligible, especially if the
guest takes his own recreational money. When we're camping, we've consistently maintained that there's always room
for one more. In our view, the primary consideration
should be whether presence of a guest will make the trip
more enjoyable for our children.

Truthfully, we've regretted taking our children's
friends camping with us on a couple of occasions. During
one three-week trip to the east coast, for example, a rift
developed between our oldest son and his best friend, and
their relationship was never the same after that. For the
most part, however, the presence of a young guest or two
has actually enhanced the trip, and we also felt good about

exposing another child to a camping and travel experience that he probably would never have had.

In our view, one very important aspect of a family camping trip is that it encourages all members of the family to spend a great deal of time together and enjoy each other's presence. Taking a child's friend along will discourage some of that togetherness; your child and his friend will tend to spend most of their time together, apart from the rest of the family. On the other hand, the presence of a guest enables the parents to devote more personal time to each other, and to the other children, without having to worry about neglecting the child who brought his friend along.

Consideration should be given to how your child and his friend will spend their days. If the trip is going to be planned around participative activities such as swimming, bicycling or visiting amusement parks, it is likely your child will enjoy those activities more with a friend. For trips where activities of a more personal nature are planned -- visiting educational attractions such as museums or taking a father-and-son fishing excursion, for example -- we recommend not inviting your children's friends along.

In any case, don't take your children's friends camping with you during your first few trips. Give your family members the opportunity to learn about each other in a camping setting without the distraction of another person.

Although our family camping style is a rather casual one, with everyone given a great deal of freedom to come and go as he chooses, we do believe in setting basic rules and adhering to them. Any young guest who goes camping with us is expected to follow those rules, too. Our rules are rather simple: curfews for each child, depending upon age; camp chores must be done on schedule; we insist upon knowing where each child is at all times, and appropriate behavior and manners are required.

Once it is determined who will participate in the trip, we can begin preparing a list of supplies and equipment that we will take with us.

Chapter 2

Costs of Camping

When we started camping with our kids, we did so not because we held such a deep appreciation for nature or the out-of-doors, but because we literally could not afford to travel as a family any other way. The cost of motel rooms and meals in restaurants, plus a week's lodging at a resort (or even in a rented cabin) was prohibitive for our young, growing family. Camping provided an economical way for us to travel together.

Our initial trips consisted basically of car-camping. That is, we slept as often as possible in our car. As the size of our family increased, we graduated to camping in a medium-size tent and then to two tents. From time to time, we rented small travel trailers and folding camping trailers for our vacations. When we could afford to do so, we bought a 17-foot Class C mini-motorhome and, from that time on, we were dedicated RV-campers, although we continued to use a tent, too.

During the last 20 years, we have camped in virtually every type of RV built -- from economy-priced folding camping trailers to $400,000 bus conversions. None has given us more pleasure than our first mini-motorhome. We bought that coach new during the Arab oil embargo of 1973-74 for $6,000. It had only a few amenities: a small furnace that worked once in a while, an icebox (not a refrigerator), a two-burner range top, and a sink with a hand-pumped water supply. It had no bathroom facilities of any kind, but its cabover bunk, rear gaucho and dinette/bed slept the six of us adequately at night.

When we stopped overnight at a campground, the mouths of other campers would drop open from amazement as, one by one, the six of us (and our dog) stepped out of that rig!

Most of our friends who also became campers during the 1960s and 1970s did so primarily for economic reasons. Doubtlessly, today's young families are considering camping vacations for somewhat the same reasons -- and because camping is an enjoyable, yet affordable, way to see the country.

INEXPENSIVE VACATION TRAVEL

A few years ago, a cost analysis of camping vacations versus other types of travel revealed that a family of four could vacation far more inexpensively by camping than by any other means. Although the analysis did not look specifically at tent camping, it did consider the cost of traveling by car towing a folding tent camper, and it concluded that that method of vacationing was the most economical type of vacation possible, regardless of trip distance, trip duration or region of the U.S.

While actual vacation costs doubtlessly have increased since the study was done, we believe the comparisons are still valid. Tent-camper vacationing for two nights cost $130, while traveling in a car and stopping two nights at motels or hotels cost $287. Cost of an eight-night tent-camper trip was $436 compared with $1,055 for car/motel travel. A 21-night trip by tent-camper was $1,082, but staying in motels and traveling by car cost $2,584. The costs of using truck campers, motorhomes or travel trailers were slightly higher than for traveling with folding tent campers, but still considerably less than stopping overnight at motels.

When the study was done, the average cost of motel rooms was $50.24 per night, and the average campsite was $10.46.

Cost comparisons do not tell the whole story, however. Traveling families also ought to consider what we refer to as the Freedom Factor. Camping families have practically unlimited freedom to go where they want and do what they desire. They can carry their supplies and food with them, or they can eat meals in restaurants if they prefer. Camping families even have the freedom to stop overnight at motels if they choose to do so! But the only choices open to non-camping families are which motels and restaurants to select among the limited number that are available to them; they can't choose not to stop at motels.

Keep in mind that while camping, your family will spend money for some items that would also have to be purchased at home: food (including business lunches and dinners at restaurants), some gasoline, entertainment, fuel or electricity for cooking and heating, household supplies, snacks and soft drinks.

Anyone considering a camping trip for the first time should recognize, however, that the costs of gasoline and campsites are not the only expenses they will face. So if vacation funds are limited -- and they always are! -- an awareness of all potential costs is desirable.

And, as with any other form of activity involving children, camping with kids is more expensive than camping without them.

SET A TRAVEL BUDGET

We recommend that young families taking their first camping vacations establish a travel budget. Doing that can actually be an enjoyable experience, especially if the kids are old enough to participate in designing the budget.

An important part of this budgeting process should be something that we neglected to do when our children were growing up -- making sure the kids are aware of how much money the family can expect to spend for its vacation. Although doing this might seem to be unnecessary and potentially worrisome for the children, many years of camping experience with kids have convinced us that youngsters who are aware of travel expenses grow into adults who are better able to control their own vacation costs. Like many other aspects of family camping, trip-budgeting is a learning experience.

A pre-trip budget should include money for most expected expenses as well as emergency funds. Actual costs will depend upon the number of family members involved, how far from home the trip is scheduled, location of the destination and length of the vacation.

For example, one of our most enjoyable family camping trips was to South Bass Island in Lake Erie several years ago when our children were quite young. The trip was relatively inexpensive, but we had two unexpected costs that strained our budget: ferry fees from Port Clinton to the island and bike rentals while on the island. A few years ago, we returned to the island, making sure we took plenty of cash with us. The island was considerably more developed, there were more tourists and shopping was more expensive. Instead of renting bikes, we rented golf carts and gave little thought to the extra money we spent. Did we enjoy ourselves more because we were better off financially? No, we didn't. The first trip was more enjoyable, and it would have been even better if our travel budget had been larger.

Based on our experience, here are the items that ought to be considered as a family's budget is prepared:

- Gasoline for the car or RV.
- Campsite fees of $15 per night.
- Food at $10-$15 per person per day.
- Highway tolls.
- LP-gas for cooking and heating.
- Campground directories at $15 each.
- Fishing licenses, tackle and bait.
- Boat rentals.
- Swimming fees.
- Souvenirs.
- Postcards and postage stamps.
- Movies and other amusement fees.
- Firewood.
- Photo film and film processing.
- Snacks, soft drinks, ice cream.
- Allowances for children.
- Ice.
- Showers.
- Meals in restaurants.
- Replacement supplies.

Although those categories should cover most expenses during the trip, they do not include the initial cost of clothing, supplies and camping equipment. For a first-time camping family, those expenditures can add significantly to a vacation's cost, although most of the equipment and some clothing and supplies can be used several years.

We will focus more specifically on clothing, supplies and equipment in a later chapter, but we'd like to recommend here that parents include the cost of a few small items in their pre-trip planning budget. We're convinced those items make camping more enjoyable, safe or educational for children, and we think they should be a part of every family's camping gear. Here are those items:

SPECIAL GEAR FOR KIDS

1. A flashlight for each member of the family. Flashlights have a way of disappearing around our house no matter how many of them we buy. We've tried buying different colors of flashlights and assigning the colors to our kids, but even that doesn't prevent flashlights from disappearing from one year to the next. We have never been overly concerned about the safety of our children in campgrounds, but even so, we insist that each child carry his flashlight with him after dark. Also buy a few extra flashlight batteries.

2. A road atlas for each child who is interested in having one. Some youngsters take absolutely no interest in the vacation route, and buying atlases for those kids is a waste of money. Generally speaking, however, children over the age of 10 or 12 often find road atlases to be useful and interesting. We strongly recommend that parents purchase Rand McNally atlases for themselves and for their children. Atlases produced by other publishers usually are not as good, especially if they list cities and towns on the

same pages as their maps; small, quaint towns that have particular appeal to children often are not listed in those atlases.

3. Provide a trip diary or log for each child who wants one. We will discuss this topic more later. For now, we'll suggest only that a trip diary is an excellent tool for kids to use in recording their daily expenses so that, at trip's end, they know exactly how they spent their money.

4. Provide each child with a good but inexpensive compass, and show him how to use it. Even if the child is not expected to go hiking or backpacking, using the compass to determine travel directions (even in the campground) will provide valuable experience in the event that a future trip does include backcountry travel or wilderness hiking.

Finally, we'd like to offer some tips on several of the budget items listed earlier.

GASOLINE -- When budgeting funds for gasoline, make certain to include money for side trips and sightseeing excursions. Generally, each side trip will not involve traveling off the planned route more than about 100 miles. Also keep in mind that side trips probably will increase your expenditures for shopping, entertainment and campsites and could result in more meals eaten in restaurants than originally planned. Side trips are often spur-of-the-moment decisions, and planning for them is a difficult but necessary part of the trip-budgeting process for families trying to economize.

FOOD -- Although meal preparation at the campsite is one of the best ways to conserve money while traveling, occasional meals eaten in restaurants that have a local flavor can add to a child's educational experience and increase his appreciation for travel. Our family looks forward to our periodic trips to the New England states partly because there is nothing we like more than stopping at the roadside lobster pounds in Maine and eating seafood two or three times a day. We also enjoy cajun cooking in Louisiana; country cooking in Kentucky, Tennessee and Missouri; fresh salmon steaks in Washington; lumberjack dinners in Oregon; thick steaks in Texas; bratwursts and cheese in Wisconsin, and walleye fillets in Minnesota.

TOLLS -- Budgeting for tolls is usually necessary, even if the family intends to circumvent toll roads and travel other routes. Toll roads are often the best and fastest ways to travel, and the family with a limited amount of vacation time should consider that to be an important factor. By all means, if the intent is to see as much country as possible, avoid toll roads and interstate highways and travel by secondary roads. But if speed is a consideration, we recommend spending the extra money for toll roads.

CAMPSITES -- Purchase of a good campground directory -- Trailer Life's or Woodall's -- is a necessary investment because it will provide your family with a broad choice of overnight and destination campsites. If you use the directory to compare campsite fees and services, you will save enough money to pay for the book. We recommend you also pick up a current copy of KOA's directory (free at any KOA park). Choose your campsites according to the fees you want to pay and the kinds of services your family will use. Paying for services you don't need is a waste of money. Sometimes a family can save money by camping a week or more at an overnight-type campground;

most park managers are willing to charge lower daily rates
to longer-term guests.

Also, we recommend use of our own directories,
Guide to Free Campgrounds and *Save-A-Buck Camping*.
The free-campgrounds book lists thousands of sites for
which overnight fees are not charged, but most of those do
not have hookups or services. The save-a-buck book lists
sites with overnight fees of $4 and under, and many of
those -- including a large number of city and county parks
-- do have hookups. The books are $14.95 and are
available in bookstores, at RV dealerships and at Camping
World outlets. Experienced camping veterans frequently
use free and low-cost campsites in order to help them conserve funds so that they can afford to stop at higher priced
full-service campgrounds from time to time.

FISHING LICENSES -- Fishing is the number one
activity of today's campers, and it is a sport that can be
enjoyed by the whole family. Fortunately, children under
16 years of age are not required to have licenses in most
states, but interstate travel means that adults must purchase
relatively expensive non-resident licenses. When purchasing fishing licenses, make sure to keep in mind how many
days you will actually spend fishing in that state. Some
states offer one-day licenses, some have three-day permits,
and most offer one-week or 10-day licenses in addition to
the annual licenses. Husband-and-wife permits also are
sometimes available. Compare the fees for the various
types of license and then ask yourself whether you probably
will fish in that state again during the current calendar year.
Sometimes an annual permit can turn out to be the least
expensive for parents who take their kids camping in
another state frequently.

FISHING BAIT -- Two enjoyable ways to save money on fishing bait are to make your own fishing lures or catch your own live bait -- with your kids, of course. Lure-making kits are available in many sporting goods stores or can be purchased by mail. Don and our sons have, for years, enjoyed preparing for their fishing trips by making their own versions of spinnerbaits and plastic worms. When Don was younger (and not so lazy), he and the boys also caught their own live bait -- nightcrawlers, redworms, crayfish, etc. A great deal of money will not be saved by making your own lures or catching bait, but both activities are quite a lot of fun and help build kids' enthusiasm for the camping trip.

BOAT RENTALS -- Renting boats at vacation destinations can be quite expensive, but there are ways to reduce that cost. One way is to consider stopping at lakeside camping resorts that provide complimentary boats to campers that rent sites for a week or longer. Even if the campground charges boat rental fees, quite often the manager is willing to accept a lower rate from his vacationing guests. A significant amount of money can be saved by taking your own outboard motor with you; a $10-per-day boat rental fee can escalate to $30 or more when an outboard motor is rented. An alternative to buying an outboard motor is investing in a small electric-powered "trolling" motor connected to an automobile battery; those motors are adequate for moving an aluminum boat around rather well on a small lake. Families that expect to do quite a lot of fishing on their camping trips probably should consider buying either a cartop boat or an aluminum boat and trailer. A trailerable boat towed by a car or motorhome can serve double duty by carrying tents or supplies.

SWIMMING FEES -- An increasing proportion of overnight campgrounds have swimming pools for which no fees are charged, although the cost of the pools is built into the camping charges. Some destination-type campgrounds -- those that appeal to vacationers but not to overnight campers -- charge extra swimming fees, however. Sometimes, families can save money by spending their vacation at an overnight-type campground rather than at a destination resort that adds charges for its recreational facilities and services. As mentioned earlier, managers of most overnight campgrounds are willing to charge reduced daily rates to families who spend a week or more in one site.

SOUVENIRS -- High-traffic tourist areas offer innumerable ways for camping families to spend money, especially on souvenirs. We strongly recommend that budget-minded families avoid shopping for souvenirs in those areas -- many of which are simply highly commercialized tourist traps. Available souvenirs are usually made poorly and overpriced, but they are attractive to impressionable, unsophisticated children. By all means, take your kids to the Sea Lions Cave in northern California, the Wisconsin Dells in Wisconsin, Fisherman's Wharf in San Francisco, Disney World in Florida, Branson, Missouri, or to Gatlinburg, Tennessee. But don't buy souvenirs there! Instead, find out where the natives like to buy their own trinkets and keepsakes. Flea markets, antique shops, crafts stores and other retail outlets that gear their business to local residents frequently offer merchandise that is well made and reasonably priced.

POSTCARDS -- Postcards are an excellent tool to use in communicating with friends and family while you're traveling. They are relatively inexpensive, and their use should be a part of the camping family's budget. However, kids have a tendency to buy postcards which bear little or no relationship to the family's vacation. Friends and family members back home would much rather receive a postcard that shows scenery or an attraction you've visited than one which features a silly cartoon and a "wish you were here" message.

MOVIES -- As any parent knows, admission fees to movie theaters are becoming unaffordable. Add the cost of a few soft drinks and popcorn, and even an afternoon movie matinee can cost a small family $25 or $30. When we're on a camping vacation, we seldom even consider going to a movie theater because there are so many other things we'd rather do. But when on extended camping trips of more than a couple weeks, we do enjoy relaxing occasionally with a good movie. Instead of spending money going to theaters, though, we now take a TV set and a VCR camping with us. Most travelers do not know it, but video rental stores in areas that cater to campers and other tourists are pleased to rent videos to vacationers.

FIREWOOD -- When we started camping with our kids, finding firewood at campgrounds was never a problem. Most campgrounds offered it free as a service, and at many, it was even pre-cut and split. Gradually, campgrounds -- and even public parks -- started charging fees for firewood, and today, it's not unusual to pay $3 to $5 for an armload. Several years ago, when our children were small and our travel budget was tight, we began taking a small supply of firewood with us when we left home. Later, we reduced this to a couple handsful of kindling to use in starting campfires, and now we don't bother to take any wood with us; we buy our firewood and kindling like everyone else. Taking wood from home, however, is not only an easy way to control camping costs, but also, if the kids have responsibility for gathering and packing the wood, it can help build enthusiasm for the trip.

PHOTOGRAPHIC FILM -- All film for a trip should be purchased beforehand from a store in your community that sells it at a good price. Make sure you buy at least as much film as you think you'll need because film is a commodity that is almost always used eventually, and film prices at tourist centers can be ridiculously high. Also, make sure you have enough cameras to satisfy your family's quest for pictures. We don't necessarily recommend providing a camera for every member of the family, but one camera for every two persons is not unreasonable. Inexpensive 35 mm cameras with built-in flash and automatic exposure controls are excellent and furnish top-quality color prints. When buying film for those cameras, don't purchase 12- or 20-exposure rolls; pay a little more and buy 36-exposure rolls -- you'll get more photos per dollar spent. How much film should you buy? Our friends in the travel writing/photography field agree there is only one reliable rule of thumb for buying vacation film: Estimate how many rolls you think you'll need, and then purchase 50% more than that! Make sure you store your film in a cool, dry place -- an RV refrigerator is ideal.

SOFT DRINKS -- Parents who go camping with kids for the first time are in for a surprise if they keep track of how much money is spent during a vacation for soft drinks. It seems as if campers, especially young ones, are constantly thirsty, and cans of soft drinks can disappear by the caseful within a couple of days. We recommend parents try something that never really worked well for us: Pack a large supply of bottled or canned juice and try to steer the kids away from consuming so much Coke or Pepsi. We suspect the primary reason that idea did not work well for us was that we did not set good examples for the kids; we chose soft drinks ourselves over juice at every opportunity. After fighting the battle for a few years, we finally gave up and started packing large quantities of our kids' favorite soft drinks. Maybe you'll have better luck with juice....

ALLOWANCES -- This is a ticklish subject for parents, no matter whether traveling is involved or not. How much money should be given to a kid to spend on his vacation? The answer: It depends. On what? On the child's age, on his expectations, on the family's financial status, and on any number of other variables. It is difficult for us even to make recommendations on this subject because, to be honest, it was an area for which we discovered no workable guidelines during all the years our four children were growing up. The only real rule of thumb we can iden-tify is that the amount of money kids spend while traveling is directly related to the types of vacations they're on -- obviously, less money is needed on a fishing trip to northern Minnesota than on an activity-filled trip to Orlando, Florida. The best advice we can offer to parents camping with their kids for the first time is this: Give them only as much money as you think they'll need on the first day and then adjust the amount each day thereafter.

SHOWERS -- We included this category as a budget item only because there are still campgrounds which charge guests for using their showers. In the late 1950s and 1960s,

it was commonplace for campgrounds to charge for showers, but that practice gradually disappeared during the last
several years. Personally, we resent having to pay to use
showers or toilets, and we now refuse to patronize a
campground where such fees are levied. But of course,
whether you do it or not is your choice....

REPLACEMENT SUPPLIES -- Beginning camping
families tend to pack more camping supplies -- especially
groceries -- than they need. We recommend that you be
careful not to overstock anything unless you are either able
to buy the merchandise at extremely low prices or a particular product with special appeal for you is not widely
available anywhere but in your hometown. For the most
part, camping supplies and groceries are priced reasonably
nearly everywhere in the country (with the possible excep-
tion of Alaska and in some parts of Canada). Overstocked
merchandise takes up valuable storage space and serves no
worthwhile purpose if it is something that can be replenished rather easily. Besides, we truly enjoy going grocery
shopping at stores near our vacation destination.

TOURIST ATTRACTIONS -- As young parents, we
always seemed to have a shortage of money whenever we
started planning our camping trips, and therefore, we constantly searched out free or low-cost ways we could enjoy
traveling with our kids. In the early 1980s, a Florida-based
writer named Mary VanMeer provided help by publishing
an excellent book for families such as ours. It was called
Free Attractions U.S.A., and it contained listings of family-oriented attractions around the country for which no
fees were charged. Miss VanMeer also wrote and published
See America Free, which was a directory of free U.S.
campgrounds. In 1986, we had an opportunity to purchase

rights to the two books from Mary, and we converted them into our own *Guide to Free Attractions* and *Guide to Free Campgrounds*. The free-attractions book has gone through several updates since then, and it now includes 640 pages of cost-free attractions. We're proud of it, and we recommend it to you and your family.

Chapter 3

Camping With Infants

Parents who choose not to go camping until their babies have grown into young children are missing out on a great deal of fun. They are also losing the opportunity to share a wonderful period of the babies' growth and learning. Babies are quite adaptable, and if appropriate steps are taken to ensure that they will be comfortable on a camping trip, they will very quickly become acclimated to the out-of-doors and to a traveling lifestyle.

The best advice we can offer parents with an infant is to avoid becoming unduly worried about everything that can go wrong on a camping trip with baby and look at the trip as a positive experience for both you and the child.

Certainly special planning is necessary, and presence of the baby will limit the types of activies, travels and destinations that can be scheduled, but going camping with a baby truly is not a great deal different from living at home day to day with a baby. And, it can be a lot more enjoyable and relaxing.

Two secrets to successful camping with an infant is to make certain the baby's personal schedule is not upset very much and that the baby is comfortable and gets enough rest. Usually, that means family members will have to schedule their activities around the baby's naptimes and mealtimes. For the most part, doing that is a matter of common sense: For example, don't plan a sightseeing excursion during the baby's regular naptime or when the baby is tired and in need of rest. Let the baby sleep and then go sightseeing. The baby will enjoy the outing more, it is less likely to be cranky, and the whole family will have more fun if the baby is satisfied and quiet.

Start your camping vacation with the attitude that the trip should be a relaxing time for both the baby and yourselves. Don't think you can pack 18 hours of activity into one day. Doing that will disrupt the baby's schedule, disturb his rest and, quite likely, make the whole trip a nightmare.

Our children have camped with us since they were babies, partly because camping was the only form of travel and entertainment we could afford and partly because we learned quickly that our children could enjoy the out-of-doors and most aspects of camping life long before they were old enough to walk.

Making sure a baby is comfortable and enjoying himself requires parents not only to adjust their own schedules, but also to pack special supplies and equipment that ordinarily would not be taken camping. Here is a short list of that equipment:

- Infant backpack for carrying a toddler.
- Chest carrier for a baby.
- Stroller that folds down into a makeshift bed.
- Playpen.

•Mosquito netting.
•Infant seat that clamps to a picnic table.
•Guard rail that fits on any bed the baby will use.

During the mid-1970s, all our camping was done with two very small children -- Sarah, who went camping with us not long after she was born, and Micah, who was only 18 months older. Fortunately, by that time our oldest son, Chris, was a very responsible nine-year-old, and he helped us watch them and also was a good companion to his five-year-old brother, Thad. As a consequence, we did not use a playpen nearly as often as we would have if Chris not been available for part-time babysitting duties.

A playpen is an excellent piece of camping equipment, however. Nothing can beat it for short-term care of infants, and it serves admirable double duty as an out-of-doors bed for both toddlers and babies. We always carried thin-screen mosquito netting which Pam attached around and over the top of the playpen with elastic to protect Sarah and Micah from insects. Makeshift awnings or large golf umbrellas provided shade for their faces and bodies while they slept. Until our children were about three years old, a playpen was a convenient tool for coralling them.

Small children of all ages -- and especially crawling-age babies -- need opportunity to move around and burn some of their stored-up energy, however. So we believe in using a playpen sparingly and allowing youngsters as much freedom as possible to explore and play. That freedom is especially important while the family travels to and from its camping destinations. Roadside rest areas in most states are excellent park-like environments in which children can play and work off energy they build up while traveling.

PLAYING IS BABY'S JOB

We've always believed a child's primary job in life is to play. And part of our responsibility as parents is to help that child enjoy his playing as much as possible. Therefore, when we stopped at parks or rest areas during our trips, we made a point of encouraging the small children to move around, exercise and play. With babies and toddlers, that usually meant carrying them or walking with them -- in effect, exploring the interesting features of the park together -- or, in some cases, playing ball (babies love to roll balls back and forth), tag or other physical games with them, even to the point of rough-housing on the ground with them.

We also believed that although we should do everything possible to protect them from danger and injury, it was ridiculous for us to protect them -- especially on a camping trip! -- from dirt. So we'd let them walk and crawl around in a park's grassy area. Or even, at times, let them play in the dirt. We always kept soft wash cloths and pre-moistened towelettes handy, and the kids cleaned up quite nicely after their playing was finished.

However, special care must be taken at all times to protect infants' skin from sun, insects, wind burn and poisonous plants.

A good sunscreen is absolutely necessary when camping with babies. We prefer using a heavy #25 sunscreen which provides extra protection from the sun's strong ultra-violet rays; some parents recommend lighter, #15 sunscreens, but we regard that as a minumum weight for children.

Also remember that the sun can be brutal on the head of a baby which has little or no hair to protect it; that means a hat should be worn outdoors by babies and small children as well. If the sun is especially bright, use large golfing umbrellas to provide additional protection while the baby plays or sleeps outdoors. The shade an umbrella provides also helps prevent a baby from overheating on a hot day. An umbrella is a handy tool for families camped on the beach, near lakeshores or in areas with heavy winds. Even on warm days, wind can blister a baby's sensitive skin, and a strategically placed umbrella can block the wind while it provides shade.

We do not recommend using commercial insect repellent on a baby's skin, but if you plan to camp in areas with heavy concentrations of black flies, sand fleas or mosquitos, you probably should ask your family doctor to suggest a repellent. Avon's skin lotion, So Soft, has a reputation for being a good insect repellent, and we've used it ourselves because of that reputation, but we cannot claim with any certainty that it discourages insects from biting.

THE COMMON-SENSE APPROACH

Obviously, there are different kinds of hazards to infants while camping than there are at home: hot coals from a campfire, sharp fishing hooks, poison ivy and broken glass. But most of those hazards can be managed the same way home hazards are managed -- by keeping potentially dangerous items out of the child's reach. Beyond that simple, common-sense approach, along with those mentioned earlier, we do not urge parents to take special precautions in protecting their youngsters. Children of all ages should be encouraged to touch and explore their environment, preferably under the watchful eye of a parent or responsible older child.

For children, nearly everything about camping is a learning experience; parents should remember that and not stifle that learning by being overly protective. Sure, the youngsters will suffer a few scrapes and bruises, and they'll get dirty. But that's why we recommend packing first-aid kits and carrying wash cloths or pre-moistened towlettes in zip-lock plastic bags.

All camping kids get dirty, and all camping kids get wet. Parents should recognize those two facts before they go camping and plan for the inevitable. Remember that small children love to get wet. They like wading in streams, crawling through wet grass, stomping through mud puddles and walking in the rain.

LET THEM GET WET!

Walking in a gentle, warm summer rain is, in fact, a pleasurable experience for everyone. So why not do it with your children? We always provided each of our kids with his or her own umbrella and rain gear (including inexpensive rubber boots for the small youngsters and cheap tennis shoes for the older ones). A small child, when carrying an umbrella and dressed in rain gear like an adult, feels more grown up if he's allowed to walk in the rain while camping. Not only is it a special occasion for him -- something his parents probably would not permit him to do at home -- but it is a learning experience too because he is able to view the wet out-of-doors as if it were a totally different world. He can watch insects scurrying for protective holes in the ground; he can see birds chirping and flying from place to place as they look for worms; he can examine rainwater flowing down the trunks of the trees, soaking the bark; he can watch rain drops bounce off the petals of wildflowers.

Recognizing that our kids would get wet on virtually every camping trip, we always packed at least two pairs of canvas tennis shoes for each child -- even the toddlers. Since we knew our kids were going to wade in streams whether or not we allowed them to do it, we decided to "go with the flow" and take them wading ourselves, making sure they did not wade barefoot, but wore tennis shoes to protect their feet. Portions of some of our most enjoyable camping trips were spent wading (the kids called it "swimming") in clear, spring-fed streams that were only a few inches deep.

One particular trip comes to mind: Sarah, who was little more than a baby, had spent a whole afternoon splashing in the water of a shallow Ohio brook. Finally tiring, she started becoming cranky, so Pam lifted her out of the water. As she frequently did at that age, she demanded to be held by her father. Pam started to give her to Don, and the moment she put her arms around his neck, she fell instantly asleep -- exhausted by her splashing in the stream but secure in her parents' embrace.

Because camping infants always get dirty and wet, parents should go prepared by packing enough clothing so that a baby can wear two changes of clothes each day, plus a possible third change if an evening restaurant meal or entertainment is planned. In addition to attracting dirt and moisture, infants tend to drool and spill food on themselves.

Youngsters also get cold quite easily, and the combination of dirt, cold and wetness add up to a need for packing at least two hooded sweatshirts for each child. We've learned that hooded sweatshirts are the most versatile type of outer garments for children of all ages -- even babies -- so we rely more heavily upon those than we do lightweight jackets. We also pack two or three swimsuits for each child as well as an assortment of caps, gloves and lightweight rain ponchos.

BACKPACK HIKING

A backpack carrier is especially valuable for parents who go hiking or sightseeing with their small chidren. Even youngsters old enough to walk tire quickly and have to be carried. A backpack carrier allows families to visit attractions that otherwise would be inaccessible because of the youngest child's lack of stamina. The backpack carrier we used when Micah and Sarah were babies was given a lot of use because at times both children were too tired to walk and needed to be carried.

But we can recall at least one time that the backpack carrier resulted in an unpleasant experience. While on a camping trip to Santa Claus, Indiana, we made a one-day excursion to nearby Lincoln Boyhood National Memorial (a very nice family-oriented free attraction). The preserved farm where Abe Lincoln grew up was a long hike from the parking area, so Don carried Sarah in the backpack. As she always did when she rode there, Sarah stroked her father's cheeks and ears with her hands. When we reached the farm, Sarah was attracted to a newborn lamb, and petted it the entire time we were there. During our return hike to the parking area, however, she once again stroked her father's cheeks and ears, and Don forgot that he was allergic to wool. Sarah's gentle caresses transferred fibers of the lamb's coat from her hands to Don's face, and he immediately broke out in a painful, swollen rash that did not vanish until we returned home a couple of days later!

Even if you take a backpack carrier on your trip, you should also, we feel, take a good baby stroller with a smooth ride, free-rolling wheels and a sunshade. Many private campgrounds and most state and federal parks have excellent hiking trails that are smooth enough for a stroller, and those trails can provide sights and experiences that are delightful for a small child or even a baby.

We believe it is important to family relationships, and to the emotional growth and education of children, that a baby on a camping trip be centrally involved in most activities. With so much usually happening around a campsite, one way to achieve that is to place the baby at the campsite picnic table in a chair that clamps onto the table. Not only can the baby watch what's going on around him, then, but he can also have his own activities and games at the table. For example, our babies enjoyed being stripped to their diapers and allowed to fingerpaint or eat messy food (such as Jello) while seated at the table. Scribbling on paper, coloring with crayons or just tearing up paper are activities that work well in an outdoor setting.

PACK SOME TREATS

Since we've touched on food, here is an appropriate place to make an important point. With a few exceptions, we recommend that camping infants be given the same food that they like to eat at home. Most baby foods travel quite well and stay fresh with a little care, and supplies of name-brand food can be replenished very easily at grocery stores around the country. We also suggest that you pack some special treats that can be given to the baby during the trip -- favorite foods or snacks that the child might not get often at home because it is hard to buy or expensive.

Finger foods and snacks should be offered to the baby during travels to and from your camping destination as well as while you're camped. Juice, trail mix and foods that are not sticky or messy are the best choices while traveling. Also remember to include foods or snacks that are good for teething if your baby is in that stage of development.

Of course, the infant's favorite toys should be taken on the camping trip, but don't forget a few other important items too: crib mobiles, the baby's favorite blanket and his familiar pillow. One item we do not recommend taking camping is an inflatable pool. We've heard parents say that a plastic pool also can serve as a temporary playpen and as a good outlet for the baby's built up energies, but our personal experience is that an inflatable pool takes up too much valuable storage space and is seldom used. Most camping areas have excellent places where a baby can play in the water, and we believe the new experience of doing that is much more valuable to the child than being able to splash around in a familiar pool.

THE BABY'S BED

Another problem to be considered when camping with infants is where the baby should sleep. While tent-camping, there are not many options: Either the parents must utilize a crib (or playpen), or the baby must sleep with one of the parents in a sleeping bag or under blankets. When RV-camping, an additional option is usually available -- most RVs, including small ones, have sleeping spaces that are suitable for babies, even if two small children must share them.

Folding camping trailers are examples of family-size RVs that have excellent sleeping facilities. The suspended, extending wing beds are quite roomy and comfortable and are spacious enough for two children or one adult and a baby. Bench-type dinettes that convert into bunks also provide good sleeping space. When we camped in our small mini-motorhome, we assigned the dinette/bunk to

Sarah and Micah, and they slept there together in their own
sleeping bags for a few years. Micah, although only 18
months older than Sarah, quickly assumed responsibility for
protecting his sister during the night, and we're convinced
that the close relationship they still enjoy today is partlydue
to the close-knit camping environment that was neces- sary
when they were infants.

No matter where a baby sleeps, however, precautions
should be taken that it not fall out of bed at night. During
our early RV-camping days, we used various kinds of
guardrails to prevent our babies from rolling out of bed
while they slept. We recommend them enthusiastically.

THE DIAPER CONTROVERSY

Finally, we'd like to say a few words about baby
diapers. When we were raising our family, there was no
public discussion about whether or not to use disposable
diapers. At that time, if you could afford to buy disposable
diapers, you did it. No one had yet voiced concern that
disposables were unsound environmentally because they
would not decompose in landfills. The disposable diapers
were relatively new on the market and available in only a
few brands and sizes, but we regarded them as a techno-
logical advancement in child-rearing. They were convenient, relatively inexpensive, and eliminated most of the
mess associated with changing a child's diapers. Those fac-
tors were quite important to us, especially while camping,
when we had two children wearing diapers at the same
time.

Like most campers, we are quite concerned about
preservation of our environment, and we feel we must do
our part in the effort to reduce pollution. But if we were
raising our family today, we honestly cannot say we would

not use disposable diapers while camping. Cloth diapers must be washed and dried, and doing that on a camping trip is not always easy. They certainly should never be washed in lakes or streams. The convenience and cleanliness of disposable diapers have to be weighed against the concern of whether or not they add significantly to our nation's trash disposal problems.

It's an issue we believe must be decided by parents on an individual basis, letting their consciences be their guides.

On Being Respectful

Family camping with infants is an excellent way to teach children respect -- respect for the environment, for fellow campers, for animals and even for other members of the family. We believe no child is too young to be introduced to the principle of respect.

An easy way to start is for parents to show their children, by example, that other family members (and, by extension, other campers) should be allowed to sleep without being disturbed. Early mornings when an infant awakens first is a good time to begin that lesson. A parent -- preferably the first one that awakens in the morning -- should cuddle with the child and either read to him, talk softly with him or play a quiet game with him.

Older brothers and sisters should be encouraged to do that too if they awaken before their parents. Each of our three oldest children assumed responsibility for keeping their younger siblings quietly entertained during our early camping years, and doing that helped build a personal bond among brothers and sisters that was evident in everything they did together.

As young children begin to learn and understand important aspects of life -- for example, that living things can be hurt -- they also can be taught to appreciate the beauty of our outdoor world. They can learn first-hand that wildflowers are pretty and smell good, but it hurts the flowers to be picked, and the flower will shrivel and die if it is not allowed to grow undisturbed. A youngster will understand when he's told the reason he should not throw rocks at birds or animals is that the rocks cause pain, and it is wrong to hurt other living creatures.

In all cases, parents should keep explanations as simple as possible, with positive action treated as important, but expressed casually and not emphasized out of proportion.

Walks around the campground, or on hiking trails, should include efforts to pick up litter, with simple explanations that litter is ugly and messy. As children grow up with that example set for them, retrieving litter and placing their own trash into suitable containers become things they do without being reminded.

Chapter 4

Trip Preparation

The success or failure of a family camping trip could very well depend upon how well preparations for it are handled during the last couple of weeks before the trip is launched. That is the appropriate time for bringing together all the details of your original planning efforts.

Please don't wait until the last minute to tie up loose ends; we've done that, and every time we've done it, we've neglected to cover at least one aspect of our trip. Usually, our omissions were rather inconsequential -- failure to pack the right types of shoes; neglecting to take rain gear; leaving a sleeping bag behind; forgetting to pack towels; neglecting to halt newspaper deliveries -- but they were bothersome.

The last couple weeks before launching the trip also is a good time to renew kids' enthusiasm for the vacation. We recommend holding a final family planning meeting at this point to discuss last-minute details. Begin by talking about how the kids view the trip, what their expectations are for it, what foods and snacks they especially want to take and the kinds of activities they want to participate in while on the road.

Planning meals for at least the first few days of travel is important at this point. We don't really recommend preparing detailed meal-by-meal menus, however. Doing that can make pre-trip grocery purchases more efficient, but based on our experiences, trying to follow a meal schedule that is prepared in advance seriously reduces a family's flexibility while traveling. Strict adherence to planned menus can quickly become a burden by forcing family members to schedule their whole vacation around meal-times. Often, the result is that food purchased with specific meals in mind is not used, and even if it is not wasted, it needlessly adds to the family's vacation costs. With a few exceptions, every camping family we've known has scrapped the meal-by-meal planning process after trying it a few times and judging it to be unworkable.

FOOD FOR TRAVELS

On the other hand, we like to prepare for a camping trip by determining the types of food we will eat during travels to our destination. Most often, we buy sliced meat -- ham, chicken breast or turkey -- at our local deli and make sandwiches during brief stops at highway rest areas. Also, since our whole family likes tuna sandwiches, we always pack several cans of that versatile, easily stored food. For meals at overnight campsites, we try to have a small but popular choice of main courses -- pre-cooked chili and taco fillings kept frozen in our RV refrigerator or allowed to thaw slowly in an ice chest; hamburger patties or hotdogs prepared over an open fire or on our portable LP-gas grill; roast beef or ham that was cooked at home, or

even a small roasted turkey that can be sliced for sandwiches.

Depending upon the type of camping trip you are
planning, a grocery list should be prepared that will meet
your needs. For example, families planning a tent-camping,
backpacking or canoe-camping trip probably should include
dehydrated, freeze-dried and condensed foods on their lists,
but RV-campers would not do that. Exactly which foods
you take with you are a matter of personal preference, but
here is a checklist of groceries for you to consider:

•Pickles	•Sugar
•Salt	•Pepper
•Ketchup	•Mayonnaise
•Mustard	•Eggs
•Butter	•Cheese
•Cookies	•Beverages
•Popcorn	•Marshmallows
•Hot dogs	•Hamburger
•Sausage	•Sliced meat
•Canned soup	•Bacon
•Tuna	•Salad dressings
•Lettuce	•Tomatoes
•Pancake mix	•Cooking oil
•Onions	•Potatoes
•Cereals	•Fruit
•Syrup	•Milk
•Tea	•Coffee
•Jelly	•Peanut butter
•Vegetables	•Desserts
•Bread	•Crackers
•Hershey bars	•Graham crackers

MEAT AND PRODUCE

During the early days of camping with our kids, we pre-cooked bulk hamburger and froze it in two-pound plastic packages. We no longer do that. Bulky packages of frozen meat do not store well, either in an RV freezer or in an ice chest, and the meat is not readily available for use because it must be thawed or re-cooked slowly before it can be eaten. The time constraint alone prompted us to pack frozen hamburger patties instead. Patties store quite easily; they can be slapped on the grill and cooked while they're frozen, and they can be used for chili, tacos or other meals the same way bulk hamburger would be used.

In our early days, we also packed enough fruit and vegetables for an entire trip, and we don't do that any more either. Quite often, the fresh fruit would spoil before it could be eaten. And, we discovered that finding locally grown produce was a very enjoyable part of our travel experience. Fruit and vegetable farmers in virtually every section of the country sell their produce at roadside stands, providing the camping family with easy access to excellent melons, tomatoes, asparagus, cherries, lettuce, corn and other freshly harvested food. One of our best camping experiences was discovering a roadside fruit stand near Lake Cumberland in southern Kentucky that sold the juiciest peaches we've ever tasted. We bought a paper bag full, ate them while traveling and then turned around, drove back to the stand and purchased two bushels more!

Fresh apples, potatoes, onions and oranges do not require refrigeration and therefore store quite easily for camping. But be sure not to pack them in plastic bags or in areas where they cannot get air; they will spoil quickly if you do. We carry ours in mesh bags, but we've talked with other campers who use old pantyhose.

Build an inventory of permanent camping supplies...

STOCKPILE SUPPLIES

At the final family planning meeting, create a list of supplies you think you will need, making sure you get input from the children. Then begin immediately to stockpile supplies. One way to do that is to place a couple of empty cardboard boxes in an out-of-the-way corner of your house and fill it with supplies gradually, using a checklist to keep account of items that are ready to go.

Because our family changed RVs quite often when we tested them for magazines, we maintained permanent boxes of supplies that we replenished as necessary and then moved from coach to coach. A family that uses one RV all the time does not need to do that; they can simply pack supplies in their RV and replenish them as needed, thus being ready to go on a camping trip virtually any time. Tent-campers are more likely to pack their supplies in boxes as we did, but those families might want to consider using sturdier boxes than those made of cardboard.

Our definition of camping supplies is any consumable item that needs to be restocked or replenished. For that reason, when our kids were small, we regarded coloring books, crayons and some types of games as "supplies." You may wish to do that too. In addition, we maintain the following list of basic supplies:

- Trash bags
- Detergent
- Toothpaste
- Bath soap
- Facial tissue
- Toothbrushes
- Zip-lock bags
- First-aid kit
- Suntan lotion
- Paper cups
- Paper towels
- Matches
- Laundry soap
- Hand soap
- Toilet tissue
- Aluminum foil
- Insect spray
- LP canisters
- Charcoal lighter
- Paper plates
- Water purification tablets

You'll notice that our list includes aluminum foil, but about the only use we have for it is outdoor cooking. We do not wrap leftover food with it any more. One reason is aluminum foil can badly blacken the interior of an RV refrigerator or an ice chest. Also, zip-lock plastic bags and sealable plastic containers such as Tupperware are much better to use in storing food.

In addition to the supplies already mentioned, we keep an inventory of permanent equipment that we do not use for anything else except camping. That equipment includes gear for meals and sleeping as well as for general camping activities. Another list consists of tools that we've found are needed while camping, and our final list is made up of clothing and personal items. Because this book is about camping with kids and not what to pack for a camping trip, we won't mention most of the items from those lists here (camping checklists are available from a wide variety of sources). However, several specific types of camping equipment are pertinent to our discussion here. They are as follows:

PERMANENT CAMPING EQUIPMENT

CLOTHESLINE -- Those of us accustomed to washing and drying clothes in our home laundry rooms might easily forget to take a clothesline camping with us. Kids' clothes get dirty and wet quickly -- and frequently -- and a 25-foot section of clothesline rope (with clothes pins) can help reduce the number of trips made to the nearest coin laundry.

ENTRY RUG -- Kids' shoes also get wet and dirty easily, and an RV or tent can become filthy unless the kids either take their shoes off or wipe them on a throw rug just inside the entry. We also place an old carpet on the floor just outside the entry. Even so, our family's long-standing rule is that shoes must be removed upon entering our RV. The kids learned to do that when they were young, and they still do it as teenagers and adults.

LAUNDRY BAG -- Few things are more useful on a camping trip with kids than a cloth laundry bag with a drawstring at the top. Several of our RVs have had built-in clothes hampers, but we still used the laundry bag in order to carry clothes to the coin laundry.

FIRST-AID KIT --More details will be provided on this subject in a later chapter, but we're mentioning it here as a reminder that a good child-oriented first-aid kit is a critical part of any family's permanent camping equipment.

FOLDING CHAIRS -- Storing them is troublesome, and there never seems to be a perfect place to carry them on a camping trip, but they should always be taken. Experienced campers seem to agree that the expensive but well-built Zip Dee spring-supported folding chairs are the best. We've used other types of lawn chairs and deck chairs, but nothing else is as comfortable and dependable. From time to time, we've tried to economize and reduce storage problems by not taking a chair for every member of our family, but we've always regretted it. Even if active kids use their chairs only a few minutes around an evening campfire, the togetherness that results is worth the expense and hassle. Folding camping chairs are especially important to have during group camping trips such as rallies or caravans. Lifelong friendships can develop during an evening spent talking around a bonfire. Quite often, chairs are required for attending RV club events such as potluck dinners, bingo parties and entertainment segments.

AX -- This is a tool no dedicated tent-camper would forget to pack, but it's one that is often neglected by RV-campers. When camping with kids, it is an important tool because campfires are an indispensable part of family camping, and a hand ax for splitting firewood is nearly always needed. We'll discuss that subject more thoroughly later.

SLEEPING BAGS -- Again, no family of tent-campers would consider leaving home without enough sleeping bags for the whole family. Sleeping bags are popular among RV campers too, but because many RVs are equipped with permanent beds, they are less important; sheets and blankets can serve quite well instead. Our experience while RV-camping with our kids, however, is that they like to take sleeping bags because the bags are quick and easy to use. They can be rolled up and stuffed into a relatively small storage space, and the kids like not having to bother with folding and unfolding blankets and sheets. Therefore, we take two types of sleeping gear on our RV trips -- sleeping bags and pillows for the kids and sheets, blankets, quilts and pillows for adults. For us, that arrangement works quite well, and everyone sleeps comfortably at night.

PILLOWS -- Each member of our family has his or her own camping pillow. Don requires two solid foam-filled pillows, and Pam uses one that is slightly softer. Pillows for the kids range from a flat, feather-filled one that is little more than a pillow case to a lumpy one containing chunks of foam. Everyone gets the pillow of his or her choice.

SCREENED DINING ROOM -- This is a piece of equipment that is especially important to tent-camping families, but it is useful for RVers, too. Set up on the campsite near the tent or RV, it not only enlarges the enclosed camping space, but it also provides a dry, mosquito-free area for meals, snoozing, family gatherings or even just to spend some time alone. Screened rooms can be quite valuable when the family camps several days at one site, but they are bulky, hard to store and carry and sometimes difficult to erect. We do not recommend their use during an overnight campout, or even for a weekend trip.

MOSQUITO NET -- Unless you either go camping with a baby or you are especially paranoid about insects, we do not recommend bothering to take mosquito netting camping with you. It's not hard to fold and pack, but it can be rather troublesome to use, and it's seldom necessary. Except for when our children were babies, the only time we can remember wishing we had netting with us was a night in northern Minnesota when swarms of mosquitos found a gap in the canvas of our folding camping trailer and tried to eat us alive!

CAMPING LANTERN -- This is another piece of equipment regarded as necessary by tent-campers but usually ignored by RV-campers. If you enjoy sitting outside your RV at night, either around a campfire or in the dark, consider trying a camping lantern (we prefer the type fueled with LP-gas canisters). It not only provides illumination, but it also lends to the cozy outdoor ambience. Camping lanterns are invaluable for families that enjoy night fishing, too.

WASTE BASKET -- We always take a waste basket on our camping trips. It really does not take up much space because other supplies can be packed inside it, and once we are camped, it serves an important function -- conveniently keeping our mealtime trash in one place. The waste basket should, of course, be filled with a plastic garbage bag. It can be kept anywhere it's needed -- in the screen room, at the picnic table if that is where meals are prepared, or on the floor of an RV's kitchen. When we go camping in an

RV, we take along a waste basket that is placed in front of the refrigerator; it is short enough so that the refrigerator door can be opened without moving it. A short, squat waste basket that will not upset easily while traveling is preferable to a tall one with a narrow base.

BACKPACKS -- There are innumerable uses for backpacks, but their primary value while camping is during family hikes with small children. Packed with snacks, beverages and nature books, a backpack can provide a child with the feeling that he is on a wilderness expedition even if he is only hiking along a campground's well-defined trail.

SCISSORS -- Every family's camping gear should include a pair of scissors. They don't have to be good ones, but they should be capable of cutting a wide variety of materials, from fabrics and thin plastic sheets to paper. You'll find an endless number of uses for scissors, especially if you fail to pack a pair!

FLYSWATTERS-- We fought biting black flies and mosquitos for a few years before we wised up and bought a few cheap flyswatters. Now, they are a part of our permanent camping gear and are always available when we need them.

SEWING KIT -- Kids that go camping lose buttons, tear shirts, rip the seats out of pants and create other forms of havoc with their clothing. A good, well equipped portable sewing kit can prevent the need for an emergency shopping trip in the middle of a vacation.

FLASHLIGHT BATTERIES -- Remember that one of our earlier recommendations was for each child to be provided with his or her own camping flashlight? Well, a fact of life about kids with flashlights is that they use batteries at an unbelievable rate. Before you leave home on your trip, buy a generous supply of batteries from a discount store. We guarantee the batteries will not be wasted.

* * *

Other permanent equipment that is important when camping with kids includes a corn popper, water jug for carrying water from home, folding table, a tent heater, cooler, dishpan and cereal bowls.

Clothing and personal items that are packed for camping are largely a matter of personal preference and quite often depend upon the family's travel habits, section of the country traveled, weather and type of camping equipment used. There are, however, important items and clothes that are easily forgotten which can make a family camping trip more enjoyable. We offer those here for your consideration:

PERSONAL ITEMS
- Shaving kit
- Trip diary
- Compasses
- Hand mirror
- Swim suits
- Swiss army knife
- Sunglasses
- Road atlas
- Cameras and film
- Portable radio
- Binoculars
- Life preservers
- Travel alarm clock
- Fishing gear

CLOTHING
- Work gloves
- Hiking boots
- Rain gear
- Headgear
- Wading shoes
- Sweaters
- Shorts
- Sweatshirts

During your final family planning meeting, discuss your vacation budget and approximately how much money each child can expect to spend. Travel diaries can be given to the children at that time, and family members should discuss how the diaries are used. In general terms, outline the projected trip, using maps and tour guides to illustrate various aspects of the route. Discuss your side trips and alternative overnight campsites, along with the activities and facilities available.

Free-lance writer Ginger Kuh, who pens a monthly "Camping Comforts" column for Camping & RV Magazine, offers this excellent planning advice:

"For the non-reading child, get picture books showing places you will be visiting. On a large piece of paper, make a list of attractions you will see and paste it on a road map of your traveling area. Place it on the refrigerator door or some other prominent place in your RV. As you journey, let them trace the day's travels with a marker and find pictures from brochures to paste next to each place on your attraction list. This will help them to remain interested in the trip and eliminate a lot of 'Are we there yet, Mommy?' questions."

When most of the trip preparations are completed, you have only one major topic to discuss with your kids: their camping vacation assignments.

Chapter 5

Trip Assignments

Before your family's final trip planning meeting concludes, we recommend making vacation assignments:

ONE -- Assign seats in the car or RV and in camp.

TWO -- Assign camp chores.

THREE -- Assign camping trip projects.

FOUR -- Assign curfews.

FIVE -- Assign last-minute trip arrangements.

In making all assignments, do so after discussing alternatives, but be flexible about the assignments and allow opportunity for changes if circumstances indicate revised assignments are desirable. Assignments should be made to preserve harmony, to share responsibilities, to foster family teamwork, to increase everyone's enjoyment of the trip and, finally, to preserve the parents' sanity!

ASSIGNING SEATS

We believe anyone who has ever driven long distances with children agrees that seat assignments are a necessary part of family travels. In an automobile's rear seat area, there are only two desirable places to sit -- by the windows. The second-worst place for kids to ride is in the middle of the back seat between two siblings and, in the case of a rear-wheel-drive car, straddling the hump. Obviously, the worst place to ride is straddling the hump in the front between two parents (unless the child is quite small, and then, riding there is considered a privilege). The driver's side rear window also has more psychological stature than the passenger side window area because that is the side of the car with control of the vehicle's destination.

Of course, if one of the parents can be convinced to ride in the rear, all the rules change. Then, the front co-pilot's position becomes the best place to ride, and the seat between the driver and the co-pilot suddenly switches from being undesirable to being quite attractive.

Traditionally, the oldest child will appropriate his or her choice position in the car if allowed to do so. Boys will almost always choose to ride behind the driver, especially if Dad holds the steering wheel. Girls will usually choose that position too, but not always; if Dad is the designated driver, daughters will sometimes opt for the window position behind Mom, who rides in the co-pilot's seat.

If you think that's complicated, just wait. It gets worse. The child who rides straddling the hump is nearly always younger than those seated next to him, but his age is unlikely to prevent him from bullying the older brothers and sisters in an effort to make them relinquish their seats to him. He will use every device he can imagine because he knows one important fact: No matter what he does or says to them, they are not allowed to hit him! If they lose control and do it, he knows he will win not only parental sympathy, but perhaps even one of the seats that he covets so much. He, on the other hand, can whisper insults to

them and touch them with his hands, feet, head and body --
and get away with it!

HOW TO BE FAIR

The whole process presents dilemmas to the parents:
how to be fair to all the kids and prevent them from fighting. The only answer is to make rotating seat assignments
so that each child gets the best seats part of the time and the
worst seats part of the time. Seat assignments also should
be made so that the two children who are most likely to
fight are seated next to each other no longer than absolutely
necessary. Prohibitions also should be invoked against one
child touching, poking, insulting, making faces at or staring
at another. Seat positions can be rotated at whatever intervals are agreeable to everyone: by the hour, by the mile or
at every rest stop.

EASIER IN A MOTORHOME

Assigning seats in a motorhome is, for the most part,
easier than in a car. The position most in demand is, of
course, the co-pilot's, and because most co-pilots tend to
leave their seat from time to time while traveling, the kids
regard it as up for grabs during those periods. Seating at
other places in the motorhome -- at the dinette, the couch
or in barrel chairs behind the co-pilot -- usually are not a
problem. Our best solution is a set of rules that states the
front passenger seat belongs to the parent who is not driving; when that parent does not want to sit there, the oldest
child is permitted to ride there for either an hour or until
the parent returns to that seat, whichever occurs first. After
the first hour, the second-oldest child gets his turn; then the
third-oldest; then the youngest. Any kid who does not want

to take his or her turn can relinquish it to the next in line, thereby simply swapping turns.

By making seat assignments at the final planning meeting instead of doing it upon departure, last-minute arguments about seating can be avoided. Don't be surprised, however, if older children negotiate their own private trades and deals on seating assignments prior to leaving home.

Seat assignments also may be necessary at mealtime in camp. Although our children have never argued over mealtime seats (at picnic tables or RV dinettes), we have talked with other parents who have had to settle such disputes. Since we've never dealt with the problem, we'd rather not recommend how assignments should be made except to suggest that you discuss mealtime assignments at your family's final planning meeting.

Discussion should also be devoted to bed assignments. Usually assignments must be made according to how many beds there are and the number and size of family members that can fit on each bed. In spite of what RV dealers claim, an RV's dinette/ bunk conversion will sleep no more than one adult or two small children comfortably. The same is true of most sofas that convert into narrow bunks, although we've used some that slept two teenagers quite well. Cabover bunks in mini-motorhomes are very spacious and can handle two adults and a small child if necessary, but swing-down cab bunks in Class A motorhomes are not designed to sleep anyone larger than an average-size teenager.

For several years, we ordered motorhomes specially equipped with facing sofas that, when converted into bunks, provided us with a wall-to-wall bed capable of sleeping two adults and two children. No other RV floor-

floorplan we ever used handled our six-member family quite so comfortably.

ASSIGNING CAMP CHORES

To be enjoyable for everyone, family camping must be a sort of team activity, with everyone doing his or her part to ensure success. Sharing campsite chores is an important part of that, and all the children should understand that their parents expect them to perform certain duties. Just as home assignments are made to kids on taking out the trash, washing dishes, doing laundry and vacuuming the floor, so too should campsite assignments be made.

We began assigning camp chores when our kids were quite young, but as they grew older, they assumed the responsibilities without being told to do it -- nearly always agreeing among themselves which chores were going to be handled by which child.

We were always quite proud of the way our kids performed in camp, especially when we first arrived. Even before we were parked, the kids were out of the vehicle, helping direct us into our site and then almost automatically performing campsite preparation duties. Other campers frequently watched them in action with amazement and then commented to us about what responsible kids we had. What the other campers did not know was that although our kids did their work so well partly because we had instructed them for years on doing it, another reason why they worked so quickly and cooperatively together was that if they wanted to go exploring, they knew we wouldn't let them leave us until the campsite was set up.

ASSIGNING THE CHORES

Campsite chores should not be assigned arbitrarily.

Assignments should be made first on the basis of who wants to do which chores. The second criterion should be which chores each child is capable of doing. But a third, and very important factor, should be teaching the children to take on new responsibilities. In RV-camping, for example, a natural tendency would be for parents to ask the oldest child to hook up the coach's water, sewer and electrical connections. But those are duties that many younger children can handle quite well if they are instructed on how to do it properly. So we often varied our kids' assignments by instructing one of the younger children to "help out" one of the older kids. At the same time, we asked the older child to teach his young sibling how to do the work.

When we first arrived in camp, our oldest son immediately assumed responsibility for helping us park and then level the tent or RV on the campsite. Since we frequently camped with both an RV and a tent, all chores related to the RV took first priority. Therefore, while the coach was being leveled, our second-oldest son hooked up the utilities. Then one or both of them would extend the awning and position a picnic table under it. Meanwhile, the two younger children were following their own assignments. One would walk the dog and the other would help make the RV camping-ready by putting an entrance mat on the ground in front of the entry door and helping unpack whatever gear or supplies the family intended to use immediately -- kindling or firewood for the evening campfire, for example.

Frequently, we stored camp chairs, a ground carpet and a folding table in a rooftop pod, and the two oldest boys had responsibility for unpacking those. Next, all the kids joined forces to erect their tent and prepare their cots, sleeping bags and air mattresses for bedtime. If we planned to use a screened dining room, they also would erect it and move tables, chairs and some mealtime gear into it.

At that point, their campsite chores were completed, but their camping responsibilities were not. Their standing instructions were to check out the campground: its shower and toilet facilities, its laundry, its activities areas, its game rooms and its recreation program. Because we always arrived at our campsite with a plastic bag full of trash, they were expected to take the trash with them and dispose of it. The oldest children assumed responsibility for the youngest ones, taking them with them as they explored. Then, after a quick examination of the campground, they were expected to report back to us, telling us about the condition of the bathhouse, the type of laundry facilities available, and any other aspects that impressed them or disappointed them.

CHORES FOR EVERYONE

Usually, we would establish a time when all the kids were expected to return to the campsite for the next meal, and we would determine if and when we would build a campfire. If we did not bring kindling or firewood with us, they would be instructed to buy it or gather it before returning. If the campground offered evening nature talks, movies or other entertainment, we would discuss whether the kids wanted to take part in them. Usually, the younger children wanted to do that, so a decision would have to be made whether they were taken to the event by an older brother or by us. When those decisions were made, all the kids were free to enjoy themselves, with the provision that the older boys share responsibility for Micah and Sarah.

No matter how old a child is, if he is old enough to walk and talk, he is old enough to handle camp chores. His assignments might be nothing more than walking the dog and cleaning up after it. Or, he might be expected to unpack all the sleeping bags and pillows and prepare them for bedtime. Maybe his only job is to keep the baby entertained while camp is being set up. The point is, he needs to feel he's an important part of the camp preparation process and is contributing to the success of the family's vacation.

When our kids were still quite young, we taught them how to make their beds, inflate air mattresses, turn on and off the RV refrigerator, open the LP-gas tanks, turn on the water pump and fill an RV's water tank. As soon as they were capable of doing it, they also learned how to convert an RV dinette, a gaucho or a dinette into a bunk, how to air out sleeping bags, how to gather firewood and how to keep a campsite clean.

One of the most gratifying experiences we had during all the years we camped with our kids came one day when we drove into a campground in a motorhome. As we approached our campsite, Chris said to Don, "Stop right here, Dad." Don did, and Chris continued, "You and Mom take a walk around the campground and enjoy yourselves. We're going to park the motorhome and set up camp by ourselves."

With a great deal of trepidation, we did as he asked and did not return to the campsite until enough time had passed for our four children to set up camp without us. When we did return, we found our kids waiting for us with big grins on their faces. They had done a perfect job of parking the motorhome, leveling it, hooking it up and making the site ready for our vacation.

ASSIGNING CAMPING TRIP PROJECTS

Kids don't often get bored while they're camping,

but it can happen, especially during a relatively long vacation at one campground. Rainy or cold weather can cause boredom, but so can camping in the off-season when activities and diversions are minimal. To prevent boredom from becoming a problem, we recommend planning for it in advance by assigning a vacation project to each child.

In some cases, the project can be a pre-vacation assignment. For example, a particularly imaginative teenager or pre-teen could be asked to prepare a collection of ghost stories that he will narrate during one of the family's evening campfire gatherings. Or, the oldest child could be asked to create a treasure hunt -- complete with clues, maps and treasures -- for his younger brothers and sisters.

Some projects could be worked on any time during the vacation that the children want to do them. If the family intends to camp on the beach, for example, one child's assignment could be to start a seashell collection, and another could be asked to collect other kinds of beach "treasures" -- driftwood, beach glass, empty crab shells, sand dollars and coral. Ocean beaches also are great places for finding different colors and grades of sand; the sand can be funneled into a clear bottle layer by layer until the bottle is filled and sealed so that the grains cannot mix together; or, different kinds of sand can be used to create sand art on cardboard sheets sprayed lightly with clear photographer mounting glue.

A LEAF COLLECTION

Another project that is popular among nature-loving camping kids is collecting leaves and pressing them for mounting in scrapbooks. Tree leaves can be identified quite easily by utilizing one of the many illustrated guide books available from libraries and bookstores.

An excellent portable leaf press can be made with simple materials, according to Susan Milford, author of *The Kids' Nature Book* ($12.95 from Williams Publishing Co., 1-800-234-8791). She recommends cutting two pieces of quarter-inch plywood or masonite into six-inch by eight-inch rectangles. Drill holes in the four corners of each board and attach them to one another with long bolts that have wing nuts. Then cut several slightly smaller pieces of heavy cardboard from an old box. Susan writes, "As you find leaves and flowers to press, place them between sheets of clean paper. Sandwich these between the layers of cardboard. Tighten the nuts evenly at all four corners to put enough pressure on the plants to press them flat. Your specimens should be dry within a few weeks."

Fossils that have been preserved in stone also can be collected by children in most parts of the U.S., Mexico and Canada. Searching through rocks along stream beds is an excellent way to begin a fossil collection. A collection of unusual or beautiful rocks can be started the same way, and in some sections of our country, valuable gems and minerals can be found.

One type of camping assignment that kids of most ages like is that of collecting items -- seashells, beach treasures or even pinecones -- that can be used later to make Christmas tree decorations. Assignments also could be part of a vacation-long contest: which child can record the largest variety of animal tracks or birds spotted during the trip, or which child can shoot the most scenic or the funniest photograph.

ASSIGNING CURFEWS

For practical reasons, we regard nighttime curfews while camping to be virtually the same as bedtime. Therefore, we assigned our kids curfews that coincided with the times we felt they should be in bed. Obviously, those curfews varied from child to child, depending upon age and our evaluation of the individual's sense of responsibility.

When we took our smallest children camping, we held rather closely to the bedtimes they were assigned at home, but with some leeway based upon the activities available in the campground. The key factor in our minds, however, was how much sleep a particular child needed each night, and that amount varied from child to child depending upon his or her energy level and metabolism.

Chris, our oldest, tended to tire early in the evening, but he would consistently try to stay active long after he should have been asleep; as a result, if we allowed him to go to bed when he wanted, he was overly tired and irritable the next day. Thad had a higher energy level but still was reasonably easy to put to bed. Micah, like Chris, tired early and was frequently the first child asleep. Sarah, who in her teenage years became a bonafide night owl, could remain active for longer periods than the rest of our children; she was not difficult to get into bed, but she did not fall asleep easily.

When stopped in a campground that scheduled nighttime activities for young children -- such as movies or costume parties -- we would adjust each night's curfews so there would be time for our kids to attend those events, return to the campsite, talk about the activities and wind down before going to bed. If an older brother were given responsibility for taking the younger kids to the event, we also would adjust his curfew accordingly so that he would have time to enjoy himself afterward. We allowed our teenagers to stay out rather late, virtually without a curfew, so long as we knew where they were. Nearly always, they spent their time either in the campground's game room, at our campsite with other kids their age, or at one of the other kids' campsite.

Admittedly, our curfew policy was quite lenient. But we believed in trusting our kids to behave and act responsibly, and so long as they did that, we did not place strict time restraints on them. The primary rule our kids were expected to follow was that no matter where they were or what they were doing, they were supposed to be quiet and not disturb other campers. Also, because Don was writing articles for national RV magazines during most of our travels, we stressed to our children that they were in the public eye and therefore, they should always act responsibly. They never disappointed us.

We usually requested all our kids to be present during family campfire gatherings, especially when we cooked hotdogs or marshmallow. Sometimes, however, we allowed the older boys to play with their friends instead. When we were camped with a group of other families and a campfire gathering was planned, we insisted that each member of our family at least put in an appearance and spend a few minutes with the group.

ASSIGNING LAST-MINUTE TRIP ARRANGEMENTS

One last bit of preparation that ought to be taken care of at the final trip planning meeting is assigning individual family members responsibility for wrapping up loose ends. Here is a list of last-minute arrangements that we recommend assigning to the kids:

•Lock all doors and windows.

•Disconnect electrical appliances (except refrigerators and freezers).

•Remove from refrigerator food that might spoil.

•Turn down home thermostat.
•Close outside water faucets.
•Empty all trash.
•Fill RV water tank.
•Turn on RV LP-gas valves.
•Turn on RV refrigerator.
•Make sure jacks, flares, lug wrenches are packed.
•Make sure tools are packed.
•Make certain all family members take their pillows.
•Arrange for someone to watch pets and water yard or plants.

There are other arrangements that only the parents should make: paying bills that might come due during the vacation period; stopping newspaper and mail deliveries; informing local police of your absence; asking a friend to check on your house periodically; checking the condition of vehicles to be used on the trip.

Chapter 6

Camping Manners

Camping vacations are an excellent way for all members of the family to enjoy themselves and escape the routines of daily life at home, work and school. But that does not mean children can or should run wild while they are camping. To the contrary; camping is more than an activity -- it is a lifestyle. And like all other lifestyles, it has its customs, its rules and its acceptable patterns of behavior. All participants, including children, are expected to follow them.

Camping manners are, for the most part, the result of simple courtesy and good common sense. They are based on the concept that everyone who goes camping has the right to privacy, safety, comfort and personal enjoyment of the outdoor environment.

The first rule of camping courtesy is to respect the other camper's rights and not infringe upon them, even accidentally. The second is to preserve and protect our natural environment so that it is available for future generations of campers to enjoy.

Obviously, children should be taught to be quiet while other campers are resting or sleeping, but that simple instruction is not enough. Most people go camping so they can enjoy some solitude; they would prefer not to be disturbed any time -- day or night. Thus, the shouting and screaming which might be quite acceptable in a child's back yard at home may not be acceptable in a quiet campground setting. For that reason, many campground managers purposely direct families of campers into one section of their park and retirees into another section. Campground activity centers are generally provided away from areas most likely to be used by solitude-seekers.

During our early days as campers, campground manners were taken for granted by nearly everyone. It was rare to be disturbed by loud music or shouting. No one talked about preserving the environment; everyone just naturally did it. Of course, there were those we called "the one-percenters" who seemed to believe they had a right to behave in any obnoxious manner they wanted, but we didn't really regard those peoples as campers, and since there were so few of them (less than one percent of the camping population, we judged), they were largely ignored.

ADULTS-ONLY PARKS

Gradually, however, the population of "one-percenters" increased, and a discouraging new phenomenon developed: Some campgrounds which had always attracted young families became adults-only parks where children were not welcome! Those restrictions were prompted by complaints from older campers that their solitude, privacy and, in some cases, safety were being threatened by rowdy children and teenagers.

Today, a large number of campgrounds in the sunbelt states -- most notably in Arizona, southern California, Texas, South Carolina and Florida -- prohibit children from camping there during the winter months when the parks are populated with retirees. We cannot blame either the campgrounds or the retirees for those restrictions, however; the fault lies with parents who allow their youngsters to misbe-

Teach children to pick up litter, no matter whose it is...

have while camping.

As parents who enjoy camping with kids, we have compiled our own set of rules and manners that we expect our children to follow. We offer them to you with the knowledge that you might want to revise them, add to them or even reject them:

•Walking across other occupied campsites is not permitted. When a tent or RV is in use on a site, that site should be regarded as the other family's property. Walk around it!

•If you see another camper attempting to park an RV or erect a tent, offer to help, especially if the other person is elderly, handicapped or alone.

•The family dog must not be allowed to roam. It must be walked on a leash, either in a designated pet area or in a grassy area as far away from campsites and foot traffic as possible. Whoever walks the dog must carry tissues to clean up after it.

•Waste water must never be dumped or flushed onto the ground.

•Campground restrooms are there for the benefit of all campers; keep them clean.

•Don't litter. If you see litter anywhere in the campground, pick it up and dispose of it properly.

•Be quiet when other campers are likely to be resting or sleeping.

•Play noisy games only in the campground activities areas, not at the campsite.

•Do not cut living trees for firewood. Do not pick wild flowers or plants.

•When wilderness camping, pack out all trash and leave the campsite cleaner than you found it.

•Do not wash dishes or clean fish in lakes and streams.

Chapter 7

The Right Rig:
A New RV or Tent

Most non-campers think choosing a family camping
rig is simply a matter of money. They believe that families
without much money go camping in tents simply because
that's all the family can afford, but that anyone who can
afford it will buy a recreational vehicle. Although there is
some basis for that kind of generality, the fact is that many
families choose to tent-camp because they love doing it, not
because they cannot afford to purchase an RV. Some families enjoy camping only occasionally and for them, a tent is
a smart investment because they cannot justify buying an
RV that they will not use often.

When prospective campers ask us to recommend
whether they should buy a tent or an RV, we respond by
suggesting they ask themselves several important questions
first because the answers will help them make the decision
without any recommendation from us. First, ask yourself
how often you will go camping. One week a year for a
vacation? All summer on an extended trip? An occasional
weekend? Vacations and weekends? Most weekends?

If your answer is that you will go camping only once or twice a year, you probably do not want to invest in purchasing an RV. Assuming that you enjoy the benefits of tent camping and are not put off by its disadvantages, buying a tent that will serve your family's needs is probably the best decision. If you do not like tent-camping but want to take your kids on camping vacations or occasional weekend trips, we recommend you consider one of three alternatives:

ONE -- Rent an RV the few times you'll need one.

TWO -- Buy either an inexpensive RV such as a folding camping trailer.

THREE -- Buy an RV-type rig that can serve other uses when it is not on camping trips. The best choices here are a van camper or a pickup truck with a slide-in camper that can be removed.

ROUGHING IT

For those families that relish true wilderness camping and like canoeing, rafting or backpacking into the boondocks where there are no other people, tent-camping is ideal. But make no mistake: tent-camping of that type is quite physical, and more than any other type of camping, it requires the participants to become part of the natural environment and share space with creatures of the night, with insects and with the weather. Call it "roughing it" if you wish, or call it "a one-ness with nature," tent camping is not suitable for families that are unwilling to put up with discomfort in various forms.

If you are considering going camping simply because you believe it is the least expensive way for your family to travel and get away from home, you probably will not enjoy tent-camping. But then again, how will you know unless you try it? We suggest you check out tent-camping before you reject it. There are two ways you can do that. One is to contact a camping outfitter and ask him to arrange a weekend campout for you, either at a campground or as part of a short canoe trip. The other alternative is not truly tent-camping, but it will give you the flavor of it: Rent one of the small Kamping Kabins offered at many of the KOA campgrounds around the country. The Kabins are basic wood shelters with walls and roofs and few conveniences; if your family members are not comfortable in one of those, they certainly will not like living in tents.

Often, one or both parents have already tried tenting and enjoyed it. They believe their kids will enjoy it too. But parents should recognize that children growing up in our material world have become accustomed to TV, VCRs, microwave ovens, shopping malls and other tools and concepts that are absolutely foreign to backwoods tent-caming. So again, we strongly suggest you take your kids on a trial campout before you invest in a tent and tenting equipment you might not use after the first trip.

Another aspect of tent-camping is that families quite often discover it does not meet their vacation needs any longer. Our family tent-camped several years and enjoyed doing it. But gradually, we moved away from it and into RV-camping because we did not wish to cope with its unpleasant aspects -- the insects, the unexpected weather changes, the packing and unpacking. Frankly, we gained an appreciation for the comforts and convenience of RV travel -- full-size beds, shelter from the cold and rain, our own private bathroom and the wonderful ability to stop briefly almost anywhere, including in highway rest areas and shopping center parking lots.

As our children became adults and left home one by

one, they returned to tent-camping, and we were glad to see them do it. But now, each of them is considering the purchase of a recreational vehicle because they do not want to continue tent-camping. Our second-oldest son, Thad, literally spends every weekend with his wife shopping for an RV. They are seeking an answer to the same question that every other camping family asks: Which rig is the best one for us?

TENT-CAMPING EQUIPMENT

Families that choose tent-camping instead of RV-camping do not really have a lot of difficult decisions to make when it comes to buying equipment. Purchasing tents actually comes down to deciding whether the whole family will sleep in one tent or in more than one. If the decision is to buy one large tent, the basic choices then are how big it should be, what it should be made of and how much it will cost. Large, rectangular cabin tents are the best family-size tents, and they are available in several sizes, fabrics and price ranges. Dome tents and A-frame tents are generally considered to be one-person or two-person structures, although new family-size A-frames are increasingly popular. Dome and A-frame tents are nearly always less expensive than cabin tents.

We are not tent experts, and the technology of tent-manufacturing has changed a great deal during the last several years, so we hesitate to recommend specific tents and fabrics for individual uses. Reputable sporting goods stores that specialize in tenting equipment, however, can offer excellent advice on prices, size and fabrics. One tip we will give you is always buy a tent that is larger than you think you will need unless you intend to use the tent strictly for backpack-camping.

When evaluating sizes, types and prices of tents, keep in mind whether most of your camping will involve stopping at developed campgrounds or in wilderness areas; whether you intend to go canoe-camping and rafting; whether you will do any backpack-camping. The ways you intend to use your tent should help determine the size and type you purchase.

Consider that once children become teenagers, they will insist upon having their own tent that can be set up separately from the one used by Mom and Dad.

AFTER THE TENT, THEN THE EQUIPMENT

Only after you buy your tent should you shop for other tent-camping equipment. The type and size of tent purchased will set the tone for your camping experiences and determine to some extent what other kinds of equipment you will need. For example, you probably will consider whether to buy sleeping cots or some type of padding for sleeping on the ground. Sleeping cots are more comfortable, but they are cumbersome and virtually impossible to carry on a backpacking campout. Also, there is a wide selection of pads available, ranging from expensive Insulite pads that are lightweight and easy to pack to air mattresses that are inexpensive but troublesome to use.

The rule to follow is, buy the equipment that will meet your camping lifestyle needs and your budget.

Some choices are not very clearcut, however. Lanterns, catalytic heaters and camp stoves are good examples. For years, we used lanterns, heaters and stoves fueled by white gasoline (also available in cans as Coleman camping fuel). White gas provides a very hot flame in a stove and a bright light in a lantern; both the flame and the light's brightness can be controlled very easily. White gas also can be used as an emergency fire-starter. The fuel evaporates quickly if it is spilled, but it is quite explosive, and cans of it are difficult to carry and can leak if they are not closed tightly.

Several years ago, we switched to appliances fueled by bottled LP-gas or butane, and we don't expect ever to return to using the other type. Fuel canisters can be purchased from most sporting goods or discount department store; they are easy to store and simple to use, and we regard them as much safer than white gas. In addition, special hose connections can be purchased allowing the appliances to be linked either to large LP tanks (such as those on the front of a travel trailer) or even to a motorhome's LP-gas tank. The only shortcomings of LP-gas is that the fuel does not light easily in cold weather, and we are uncomfortable with disposing of an empty container by throwing it in the trash. Also, there is no way to measure accurately exactly how much LP is left in a used canister (one lasts about six hours), but we regard that as a minor inconvenience.

Choose whichever type of stove, heater and lantern makes you comfortable, but we strongly recommend against buying appliances fueled by kerosene. It is a dirty, smelly fuel that has no advantages, not even producing a high flame.

CHOICE OF SLEEPING BAGS

Sleeping bags are an indispensable part of tent-camping. Again, buy those that fit your family's specific needs -- lighter weight bags for backpacking and heavier bags for other types of camping. Four to five-pound bags are regarded as the best all-around weight for anyone except backpackers. We strongly support purchasing bags that are rated for colder weather than you think you will experience on your trips. Bags rated for zero or 10 degrees above zero serve most vacation and weekend campers quite well, and they provide an extra measure of warmth not available with bags rated for only 30 or 40 degrees.

Sleeping bags filled with down have a wide reputation as being the most comfortable, but that is not really true. Down bags can become uncomfortably hot inside, even during cold weather, and if down ever gets damp or wet, it can turn a soft sleeping bag into a lumpy, uncomfortable one that is quite difficult to dry out. The natural feathers of goose down have been successfully improved upon by modern polyfibers which hold their shape even when wet and which can be dried quickly and easily. Bags filled with synthetic fibers are also less expensive than down-filled ones, and we see no reason to spend extra money for camping gear that has shortcomings.

In Chapter 4, we provided a list of permanent camping equipment that should be purchased and kept ready to go. Here is other tenting equipment that families ought to consider buying after they have purchased their tents, sleeping gear and appliances:

- Ice chest
- Ground cloth
- Saw
- Folding table
- Cooking pots
- Fire starters
- Hot pads
- Camper's pressure cooker
- Water containers
- Portable toilet
- Shovel
- Cooking utensils
- Coffee pot
- Potato peeler
- Cooking glove

One final suggestion about camping equipment: Although the boxes in which equipment is purchased is a good place for storing the equipment between camping trips, do not make the mistake of taking the boxes camping with you. Once the gear in them is unpacked, the boxes become troublesome pieces of worthless cardboard that tend to float around the campsite get- ting in everyone's way. Leave the boxes at home!

RVs AND RV EQUIPMENT

Selecting the right RV for your family is considerably more difficult than choosing a tent because there is a much larger range of types, sizes, prices, floorplans and furnishings. The choices can be narrowed for you, however, if you answer the following questions:

1. How much money do you plan to spend? Consider price ranges starting under $10,000 and increasing in $10,000 increments up to $80,000.

2. Do you have a vehicle for towing an RV? If so, what kind of vehicle is it and what is the maximum weight it is rated to tow? If not, do you plan to buy a tow vehicle?

3. How many kids will go camping with you and how old are they?

4. How will your family use the RV? Will you go camping on weekends, take week-long vacation trips or travel with it for one to three months at a time? Will you use it on flat terrain or in the mountains? Will you camp at developed campgrounds or in the wilderness where no facilities are available?

NOW NARROW YOUR CHOICES

Answers to the first question are critical in determining the type RV you should buy. Your options range from pickup camper and folding trailer to fifth-wheel, travel trailer, mini-motorhome and Class A motorhome, along with a few other types. But although you can pur-

Folding camping trailers offer spacious camping at a low cost...

chase a very nice pickup camper or folding trailer for under $10,000, you cannot buy a new motorhome or even a mid-size trailer for that amount. Even if you want to spend only $9,000 for an RV, that does not necessarily mean you are limited to a camper or a fold-out, however. A few RV manufacturers are building small travel trailers and fifth-wheels that retail for that price, and good used RVs are available for $9,000 that originally cost at least twice that amount.

Let's assume your price limit determines that your best options are a pickup camper, a folding trailer, a used travel trailer or a used fifth-wheel trailer (an outside possibility is a motorhome that is several years old and in relatively poor condition, but we do not suggest you consider that type vehicle). Now, to narrow those options, answer our second question. If your only vehicle is a car or van rated to tow under 5,000 pounds and you do not intend to buy a vehicle that can tow something larger, you have just eliminated the pickup camper and used fifth-wheel from among your options. We can see that you need to choose between a folding camping trailer and a used travel trailer.

The size of your family could help you with that choice, but if you have only one or two children, it is very likely you can find either a folding trailer or a used travel trailer that will fit your needs and your budget. So ask yourself the fourth question: How will your family use the RV? A folding camping trailer is quite satisfactory for weekends or week-long vacations, but we do not recommend it for family trips of a month or longer duration. Since you do not expect to travel with your kids for the whole summer, your options are still open. But if you plan to go camping in the mountains, we suggest you give the folding trailer your first consideration because your family car is not really equipped for towing a heavy travel trailer in mountainous terrain.

Both a camping trailer and a travel trailer could be used satisfactorily in either developed campgrounds or in the wilderness, but unless you are experienced at camping without bathrooms, electricity and running water, the travel trailer would better fit your needs. The travel trailer also is more comfortable under cold-weather conditions.

Once you have narrowed your options to one or two types of RVs, you should consider their size (towing weight and length), their floorplans (bathroom, dining space, sleeping space, storage areas) and their equipment and features (refrigerator, furnace size and location, water heater size, air conditioner, awning). You want an RV that will serve your family easily at both mealtime and bedtime. Those attributes are critical, and some RVs that are designed to sleep six will handle only two or three persons at mealtime.

The refrigerator should be large enough to cool a two or three-day supply of food for your family; the furnace should warm the whole coach on a 30 or 40-degree day, and other facilities should be of a size and type to fit your family's needs. Keep in mind what we said earlier about convertible RV bunks: a dinette/bunk, gaucho and most sofa/bunks can handle only one adult or two small children; a cabinet-bunk will serve one child at night.

Here are other aspects to consider when buying an RV:

QUALITY -- How well built is the unit?

SERVICEABILITY -- Where will you get it serviced? Is it built by a major RV company that warrants its construction and equipment? Is it equipped with name-brand appliances for which replacement parts are readily available?

VALUE -- How well will it retain its value, and will it have a high resale value after you use it a few years?

PERFORMANCE -- How well does it drive or tow? Does it corner well and is it easy to maneuver? Does it sway and feel as if it will tip over?

CONSTRUCTION -- What type of structure does it have? Those with steel and aluminum frames generally are better built, but they also are more expensive than wood-frame coaches.

FLOORPLAN -- Is the floorplan a popular one or an unusual one that might be difficult to resell in a few years?

THE DEALERSHIP -- How good is the reputation of the RV dealership where you are considering buying the unit? Does it do a good job of servicing its customers? Are its repair prices fair?

THE BRAND -- Is the coach built by an RV manufacturer that is still in business and has a good reputation, or is it an off-brand model produced by a relatively unknown company that might be out of business next year?

Where can you get answers to all these questions? We strongly recommend that you talk with friends who already are active RV-campers. RVers are a close-knit fraternity with an informational grapevine that stretches from coast to coast. They talk about their RVs at every opportunity, and they tell each other what they like and don't like about their rigs, their manufacturers and their dealers. A good friend who knows your family members also is an excellent person to advise you on RV floorplans, appliances, towing weights and other features.

After you talk with a few friends, prepare a checklist of the types of RVs that you believe will meet your family's needs and plan a family fact-finding outing to a locally held travel and vacation show. Usually, those shows are sponsored by a local RV dealer's organization and include representative models of most popular brands. RV shows are especially good places to visit just before a purchase is made because nearly always, dealers post below-normal special prices in order to attract as many potential buyers as possible.

One final recommendation about purchasing a new camping rig, whether an RV or a tent outfit: Before you leave home on a long family camping trip, take the new rig on a shakedown outing to a nearby campground for a weekend. Do that with the fullknowledge that you'll discover some shortcomings or problems that you did not know existed. You'll have time to correct the problems or get repairs made before your vacation.

Chapter 8

Other Types
of Camping

When our family switched from tent-camping to RV-camping, we sometimes felt a little embarrassed to talk about our new camping experiences with our old tent-travel compan- ions. The reason is clear: During one of our first discussions with them about a trip in the RV, we empha-sized the rig's comforts and our happiness at being able to sleep on a soft bunk instead of on the hard ground, and a friend responded, "Yes, but that really isn't camping, is it?"

Since then, we've heard similar remarks directed at RV-campers by tent-campers -- and even by owners of fol-ding camping trailers. Perhaps that is one of the reasons why RV-campers have virtually stopped referring to them-selves as "campers" and now call themselves "RVers" -- a term that did not even exist prior to the mid-1970s.

Well, we're dedicated "RVers" now, but when our family travels, we don't go "RVing." We go "camping."

Tent-camping, RV-camping, van-camping or station wagon tail-gating: It's all camping, and we feel a kinship with anyone who does it.

One of the most wonderful aspects to the camping lifestyle is that it can be enjoyed in so many ways. For several years after national RV clubs started to become popular, members of those organizations refused to take part in any travel experience unless they could do it in their RVs. Today, those same people are more adventuresome; they'll travel by RV to California and then hop an airplane to Hawaii for a rally with other club members; they'll go camping through Europe, but in a tiny rented motorhome, not the familiar, spacious one they own; they'll take club-sponsored excursions to Australia or Russia; they'll even park their RVs for several days and take an ocean cruise.

Tents and RVs are just tools, after all. They provide us with living space so that we can enjoy our travel adventures. And we're all making a mistake if we neglect to expose our children to a wide range of camping activities that might mean leaving the family tent or RV at home.

While you are planning a camping trip with your kids, we recommend that you consider introducing them to one of the "other" types of camping: backpacking, houseboating, canoe-camping, Kamping Kabins, renting an RV, renting a tent, rafting or float-tripping, camping club rallies, RV caravanning or group camping.

BACKPACKING

Backpacking is probably the most basic of all camping experiences because it involves self-mobility and a higher degree of both self-reliance and teamwork than most other methods. Not only must participants carry all their supplies, equipment and shelters on their backs, but they also must share the load and cooperate with each other in order to make the experience safe, trouble-free and enjoyable. Backpacking allows partici pants to view our natural environment from a perspective that is not available from the window of an RV or the game room of a private campground. It also opens up areas of our country that cannot be reached by automobile or motorhome.

In the 154 national forests administered by the U.S. Department of Agriculture, more than 1 million miles of trails lead backpackers to tiny, unnamed lakes fed by permanent snowfields; boulder-strewn canyons; alpine meadows; cool, cathedral-like stands of pine, and granite peaks high above the timberline. Some 181 million acres of national forests are open to the backpacker, including 9.1 million in national wilderness areas. Another 22 million acres of national parks and monuments, 5 million acres of state parks and 17.5 million acres of state forests are also available to the camper.

Young camping families do not have to hike into the unexplored wilderness in order to share an enjoyable backpacking experience, though. Backpacking also does not need to involve hiking long distances. When backpack-camping with kids, a short hike often is more desirable. In addition to the public lands mentioned earlier, camping families have the benefit of formal hiking trails provided by many private campgrounds. Those trails are well defined, and quite often, the campground management has gone to the trouble of marking trees, plants, wild flower beds and geologic formations with identifying legends to make hikes more educational.

If your family does not have overnight backpacking equipment, a check with camping outfitters (or even sporting goods stores and equipment rental companies) in the area you are vacationing frequently will turn up the availability of gear that you can rent. If your family has lightweight tent-camping equipment already, you might be able to make it suffice during a short hike and one or two nights sleeping under the stars. For your first backpacking experience, hike into the woods a couple of miles, making an effort to reach an area that is relatively secluded from jogging or hiking traffic. That small taste of backpacking ought to provide your family with enough experience to decide whether or not a longer, more adventuresome trip should be planned in the future.

For a listing of national forests and information on camping and hiking in them, write National Forest Service, U.S. Department of Agriculture, Office of Information, Room 3219-S, Box 2417, Washington, D.C. 20013. For an introduction to national parks and the facilities they offer, send for The National Parks Camping Guide or the National Park System Map and Guide, National Park System, U.S. Department of Interior, P.O. Box 37127, Washington, D.C. 20013-7127. Developed and undeveloped public campsites suitable for backpackers are among the entries our own popular guidebooks, *Guide to Free Campgrounds* and *Save-A-Buck Camping* ($14.95 each from bookstores or Cottage Publications, 24396 Pleasant View Dr., Elkhart, IN 46517).

HOUSEBOATING

Houseboat vacations are an especially enjoyable way to take kids camping. In fact, no other form of camping can duplicate the types of experiences that are possible during several days aboard a houseboat. Kids who enjoy seclusion and serenity but like to mix in fishing, exploring, water sports and even shopping can do all that -- and more --

while houseboating.

Most houseboat rental docks are located on very large, heavily used lakes such as Lake Cumberland in Kentucky and Lake Powell in Utah. Thus, houseboating can be done either in the middle of crowds of other families or in total seclusion at the upper end of a small bay. Some other lakes, such as Rainy Lake (which straddles the Minnesota/Ontario border) appeal primarily to fishing families and those who want to escape into the wilderness.

Most houseboats are equipped similarly to a large travel trailer, with sleeping quarters, a kitchen and dining area, a bathroom and storage space. In addition, a typical houseboat has a large open-air deck that is great for relaxing and a rooftop access that is a ideal for sunbathing. By towing a small boat with an outboard motor behind the houseboat, a family has total freedom to explore or fish any section of the lake easily.

We have rented houseboats only a couple of times, but we've also taken RVs aboard the large floating cruisers operated by Camp-A-Float, and we definitely recommend that method of camping as a good change of pace. Children enjoy the sense of freedom and independence that goes with houseboating.

When Don was young, he and his father went houseboating each year on Rainy Lake with ten other men and boys. No females were ever invited on those trips, which were scheduled strictly as fishing vacations. The fishermen rented two houseboats and six aluminum boats with motors. They crossed the Canadian border from International Falls and tied the houseboats to shore in the middle of some of the best game fishing waters of North America. Using the houseboats as a base camp, they explored wide areas of the lake in the two-person aluminum boats and

Canoe-camping can involve either a tent or an RV...

then returned to camp in the evening for a feast of fresh fish. Don recalls those trips as among the most enjoyable vacations he ever took.

CANOE CAMPING

Americans are fortunate to have thousands of streams and lakes that are suitable for canoeing and overnight shoreline camping. The Boundary Waters Canoe Area of Minnesota is, of course, world famous for its canoe-camping, but most other states also have excellent canoe waters. For a camping family seeking a different type of adventure, canoe-camping is a perfect activity. Canoeing is enjoyable for children of most ages, especially if they are old enough to help paddle, and a whole family can go on a canoe-camping trip literally without investing any money in equipment.

All popular canoe waters are serviced by liveries and

outfitters that will rent families all the equipment necessary for canoe trips. Family members don't really have to buy anything special to participate in a canoeing adventure; most outfitters will even supply food and cooking gear. Our recommendation is that you contact a few different outfitters in the area you want to visit and ask them for details about the services they provide; then choose the outfitter that you think will fill you needs best at the price you can afford.

We do suggest, however, that inexperienced canoeists prepare for their adventure by enrolling in a brief course on the basics of canoeing sponsored by your YMCA, community college, local recreation department or similar public agency. Our family took part in a one-day instruction period several years ago, and it was an enjoyable experience for all of us even though we did not follow it up with a canoe-camping trip.

We also recommend that you schedule your first canoe trip as a one-night or two-night float in case one of your family members decides he or she doesn't want any part of canoe-camping in the boondocks. Remember that packing gear for a canoe trip is quite different from packing for other types of camping; close attention must be given to preparing waterproof packages of gear that not only will stay dry but also will be easy to unload and carry when setting up camp or portaging.

KAMPING KABINS

The Kamping Kabin concept created by Kampgrounds of America (KOA) offers the aspiring camping family an ideal method of experiencing the camping lifestyle without investing in a tent or RV. Additionally, the Kamping Kabins effectively expose families to the activities, facilities and companionship of a typical developed campground setting that is both comfortable and safe. KOA initiated the Kamping Kabins several years ago at a few select company-owned parks, but by early 1992, approximately 400 KOAs around the country participated in the program.

For camping purists, a Kamping Kabin is probably regarded more as an inexpensive motel substitute than a facility for introducing people to the camping lifestyle, but we don't agree. The small one- or two-room log structures allow families to travel in about any section of the country inexpensively and still experience most of the benefits of stopping at a developed campground. While it certainly is not "roughing it," utilizing Kamping Kabins is, in many ways, more closely related to tent-camping than is RV-camping.

A typical Kamping Kabin consists of a single room containing a double bed and a set of bunk beds. It has air-conditioning and baseboard heating for comfort, a hardwood floor, electric lighting, windows, an outside picnic table and a locking door for security. Each family supplies its own sleeping and cooking gear. Access to the campground's restrooms and showers, laundry, store, pool, playground and other facilities is included in the cost of the Kabin, which typically is about $25 per night. New Kamping Kitchens also are provided at several KOAs, and a growing number of the parks now offer Kamping Kabins with two rooms.

In order to attract more families to KOAs, and to the Kabins, the campground chain recently asked its park managers to waive overnight fees for children. By early 1992, more than 65 campgrounds allowed children to camp free. Kamping Kabins are nearly always available at the KOAs, but reservations of two to four weeks in advance are often necessary at parks located in popular tourist areas.

RENT AN RV OR A TENT

Another good way to go camping with kids the first time is to rent a tent or RV. In fact, if you do not wish to invest in a tent or RV of your own, you could schedule all your family travels around the rental of equipment. As mentioned earlier, camping trip outfitters (particularly in canoeing areas) and some outdoor equipment rental companies rent tents at very reasonable fees, and some can even provide a full range of camping equipment. In addition, some state park divisions have special "rent-a-camp" type programs meant to encourage families to use the state park and forest systems. Because those programs come and go, we hesitate to recommend specific ones to you except to note that they are particularly popular in the Midwest. We have even heard of county and municipal recreation departments that furnish overnight camping equipment to local residents for a small fee.

RV rentals are widespread and increasingly popular. Current models of motorhomes are offered through the national Cruise America system and in Canada by Go Vacations Ltd. Individuals who rent out their personal RVs and dozens of RV dealers around the country also offer a wide selection of RV types and sizes for rent. Check your local newspaper classified ad section to determine the types and prices of rentals available in your community. Here are toll-free numbers of the national rental companies: American Safari National RV Rental in Atlanta, 800-327-9668; Bates Rent-A-Home in Las Vegas, 800-732-8822; Cruise America in Miami, 800-327-7778; Go Vacations in Ontario, 800-387-3998; Holiday RV Rental/Leasing in Orlan-

Authors planned summer family camping trips around club rallies...

do, 800-351-8888.

CAMPING CLUB RALLIES

For families that enjoy making new friends and sharing their travel experiences with other people, today's camping clubs have a great deal to offer. Most clubs promote fellowship among their members by holding regular campouts or rallies around the country. There are camping clubs to fit anyone's tastes and lifestyles, ranging from those strictly for retirees, for single travelers, for military veterans and for physically handicapped persons to those which are open only to backpackers, owners of motorhomes or owners of a particular brand of recreational vehicle.

Examples of good family-oriented camping clubs include the highly regarded National Campers and Hikers Association (NCHA), the International Travel & Trailer Club, Family Motor Coach Association (FMCA), Escapees

Teens attend a dance at their RV club's rally...

and, of course, the Good Sam Club, which numbers some three-quarters of a million members. Families that own RVs, however, can take part in rallies, trips, caravans, campouts and other activities sponsored by private clubs organized especially to promote specific brands of RVs. There are clubs for owners of Winnebagos, Airstreams, Holiday Ramblers, Kountry Aires, Jaycos, Starcrafts, Shastas, Coachmen, Georgie Boys and a seemingly endless list of other RV brands -- including some brands that have not been built for several years!

Typically, an RV club rally is held at a campground, fairground or other location capable of handling the number of families who will attend. A state rally of a factory-sponsored club might attract only two dozen families, while a national rally of the Family Motor Coach Association could be attended by 3,000 or 4,000.

Rallies are excellent events for children to enjoy themselves, experience new locales and form new friendships with other camping youngsters. For many years, our family attended rallies of the Good Sam club and several factory-sponsored clubs as we traveled and wrote about camping for national RV magazines. In 1979, we became honorary members of the Holiday Rambler RV Club, and for the next dozen years, we took our children to every international rally and to several state and regional rallies of that club. Our kids made so many friends within the organization that one year when we decided not to attend a rally, even our teenagers cried about it, and we changed our minds about skipping the event.

Each summer during the late 1970s and the 1980s, we planned our summer around travels to the destination of an RV club's rally. As a consequence, we toured sections of the country that otherwise, we probably would not have visited. Those rallies took us to the Pacific Northwest, Texas, Minnesota, Nova Scotia, Pennsylvania, Vermont, Montana, Kansas, Arkansas, Florida and all of the surrounding states. Before they were high school age, our kids had camped nearly everywhere in America except Hawaii and Alaska and had traveled through most of the Canadian provinces. They made new friends nearly everywhere they went, and so did we. Some of the best friends our family has today are people we saw only once a year when we traveled and camped together.

A great deal more than socializing takes place at camping rallies, however. Attracting families to rallies is so important to most clubs that a wide series of events and activities are planned around keeping children active and entertained. A look at a recent FMCA rally in South Bend, Indiana, provides a good example of how that is done.

FMCA plans activities for three age groups of children -- it calls them TOTS (youngsters ages 2-6), TWEENS (children ages 7-12) and TATS (for Teen-Age Travelers ages 13-19). Three days during the mid-summer rally, the TATS, TEENS and their adult chaperons visited a nearby water park where they enjoyed water slides, pedal boats, volleyball, miniature golf, a video arcade and swimming. An Olympic-size pool at the University of Notre Dame was open to all kids every day of the rally, and special swimming activities for TWEENS were scheduled for an hour each afternoon. Aerobics lessons and light breakfasts were provided for the TWEENS every morning. Tuesday, the TATS and TWEENS went roller skating in the afternoon and attended a light show and musical entertainment that evening; Wednesday, they were taken to an activities park; Thursday, they organized teams and competed in field events before meeting to plan events at the following year's rally. Meanwhile, TOTS took part in activities ranging from making farm animals out of Play-Doh to watching videos and being entertained by jugglers, magicians and clowns.

For a complete list of camping clubs and how to join them, write to the Recreation Vehicle Industry Association, PO Box 2999, Reston, VA 22090-2999.

CARAVANNING AND GROUP CAMPING

One of the most enjoyable ways to go camping with kids is to join several other families in a caravan from one destination to another and spend evenings camped together as a group. We have never caravanned with other families of tent-campers, but we have participated in numerous RV caravans, and they have resulted in many of our most delightful travel experiences. They also are the types of trips our children mention most often now when they recall our most active family camping years. We see no reason why families of tent-campers cannot enjoy the same types of caravanning and group camping trips that we take part in with RVs.

Our first caravanning trip was in the mid-1970s when the top executives of Holiday Rambler Corporation invited our family and those of the publishers of *Trailer Life* magazine to join them on a four-day test trip from Indiana to Ontario, Canada. The company provided motorhomes, travel trailers and tow vehicles for about ten families, and we used the trip not only to learn to know each other better, but also to check out prototype accessories, ·equipment and construction techniques that the company was considering introducing in its next model year.

The friendships that resulted from that trip have proven to be long-lasting ones, and the journey also convinced us that camping experiences are better when they are shared with good friends. During the years that followed, we took several more trips with various members of that group. We also started joining several families from the Missouri and Arkansas region as they returned home each summer following national camping club rallies; six or eight families set a tradition of spending two to four weeks together camping our way through one section of the country or another. At times -- for example, when we traveled from West Virginia to Knoxville, Tennessee, to attend the World's Fair -- the caravan totaled as many as three or four dozen look-alike recreational vehicles filled with families and couples of all ages.

Camping caravans are an especially good way to explore the country because someone in the group always has a good idea for an activity or an attraction to visit that could result in a truly wonderful experience. A few years ago when we caravanned down the Pacific coastline, one of the caravanners suggested we stop along the Rogue River long enough to ride a mail boat upriver into the Oregon wilderness. We did it, and it was tremendously enjoyable -- something that we'd recommend every family do at least once.

Caravans of RVs are a lot of fun -- and quite impressive to other motorists, too -- when participants travel together, communicating with each other via CB radio, stopping at roadside attractions and parking at campgrounds overnight together. But one of the advantages of caravanning with good friends is that they don't have to stay together all the time; each family can venture off alone and explore. Our own group's annual caravans have always been quite loosely organized. We usually select a specific destination campground where we agree to meet a few days in the future, and that allows any family to leave the caravan, travel on its own and rejoin the group at that park. At any one point during a trip with the group, the actual caravan could consist of up to ten RVs or just a couple. Occasionally, we'll even meet a family of strangers on the road, become acquainted with them and invite them to join our caravan!

Although our game plan usually calls for us to camp at private campgrounds that provide a good range of facilities at a reasonable price, we have sometimes stopped at quite expensive camping resorts, and occasionally we've overnighted in very rustic, undeveloped settings. Once in Traverse City, Michigan, we camped in a large, open field without benefit of hookups except for a single water hose that the campground extended for us. We parked our eight rigs in a large circle and then prepared a huge feast in the center, loading our folding tables with fresh fruit, vetetables and other locally produced food that individual families purchased as they traveled during the day.

After the meal, we built a fire and sat around it swapping stories and catching up on the news about each other. Not surprisingly, most of what we talked about related to camping with our kids and with friends. At one point, conversation lagged, and two dozen of us -- parents, kids and a few older couples -- sat silently for a few minutes. Then, from over near the campfire, came the soft voice of a child saying simply, "This is the most fun I've ever had."

Chapter 9

Packing For the Trip

The last few days before you leave home to take the kids camping have arrived. This is the period when excitement builds and the whole family grows more and more impatient to go. But one of your most important preparation stages still remains: packing for the trip. Depending upon how you approach it, packing can be either a fun-filled procedure that leads naturally to departure day or it can be a horrendous drudgery that is marked by lost tempers and threats to cancel the whole trip.

By now, your kids should have made their own checklists of equipment, supplies, food, clothing and games that they want to take with them. And, you should have checked those lists to make sure they were reasonable but complete. The family also probably has a few loose ends to tie up before the actual packing can begin: buying food, some clothing, special camping equipment, supplies and maybe a few new sets of linens -- towels, wash cloths, sheets, pillow cases.

Buying your trip's stock of food is not as simple as going to the supermarket and bringing home groceries. As we advised earlier, you should not overstock your supply and pack food that will take up valuable space but not be used; on the other hand, you should be certain to purchase all necessary items so that you do not have to visit a store each time you stop for the night. Food on the road is not usually much more expensive than that purchased at home, but you're not going on vacation to spend part of every day shopping for groceries!

Also, it is indeed possible to save money when you buy your food supply. For example, recognize that your family will drink more beverages while camping than they ordinarily do at home. Remind yourself of all the soft drinks, shakes, coffee and juices that family members buy at work, school and restaurants each week. The cost of those beverages are not coming out of your household food budget, but a considerable amount of that money can be saved by carrying a suitable supply of beverages on your trip with you. An important fact about camping and travel is that any funds that do not have to be spent in restaurants -- particularly in fast-food outlets -- is money saved.

BUY IN BULK

Just before we pack for our trip, we go grocery shopping armed with a list of items that we can buy in large quantities. We don't do that shopping at our neighborhood supermarket, though. Instead, we visit a nearby warehouse grocery outlet or discount store that allows consumers to save money if they buy in bulk. There, we purchase food and drinks by the case -- in quantities that we are certain will last our entire trip. If necessary in order to get the best discounts possible, we purchase more than we think we'll need because what we don't take camping with us will certainly be used after we return home.

In addition to soft drinks and juices, bulk purchases can be made of toilet tissue; paper towels; paper plates; plastic bags, and canned fruits, vegetables, soup and meat such as our favorite tuna. Several experienced campers have told us they also save considerable amounts of money on their food supplies by purchasing extra-large, commercial-size containers of sugar, pickles, mayonnaise, ketchup, jelly, peanut butter, coffee, tea, chocolate, cooking oil, pancake mix, soup, laundry detergent, popcorn and other items. They take those containers home, repackage the contents into smaller quantities for the trip and store the rest in their home pantry.

In our community, a store that specializes in supplying paper items to businesses offers huge discounts to anyone willing to buy bulk quantities of paper towels, paper plates, paper or plastic cups and bowls, ballpoint pens and a wide range of other items that are useful in camp as well as in an office.

TENT-CAMPING FOOD

Unfortunately, backpackers and tent-campers who travel by car have fewer options in their purchases and packing than RV-campers -- partly because their on-the-road storage space is more limited and partly because they use somewhat different kinds of food than RVers (experts recommend that each backpacker should plan on carrying about 1.5 pounds of food per day). Even so, by shopping carefully for their food, they also can save money. Families that are totally committed to tent-camping or backpacking also should buy bulk quantities of canned goods at discount prices; they can set aside most of it at home for future camping trips and pack only enough to fill their immediate needs during the trip ahead.

Most warehouse and discount stores sell condensed juices and dehydrated soups, and some even stock supplies of asepticly packaged milk, meat (beef stick that does not need refrigeration, for example) and full meals. The weight-conscious backpacker can purchase large boxes of oatmeal, rice or pasta and, like our RVing friends, repackage the contents in small quantities for easy handling. Special food items such as sun-dried tomatoes and fruits that need to be reconstituted with water usually must be bought at sporting goods stores or backpacking shops. The stores charge premium prices for those special foods, but sometimes money can be saved by shopping in the off-season and during periods the stores are trying to build consumer traffic by offering discounts.

Off-season purchases of other gear can provide additional savings for all campers. Shop for kids' games, for example, after the Christmas season; buy linens during department store white sales; purchase fishing and camping gear in the fall; build your inventory of soft drinks every time stores offer unusual discounts in order to attract shoppers; watch for savings on crayons and paper during late summer sales of school supplies.

CLOTHING FOR ALL OCCASIONS

Nothing is more frustrating than to go camping and discover that you did not pack the appropriate clothing. For most campers who travel during the summer, that usually means failing to take clothes for either unexpectedly cold or exceptionally hot weather. In some cases, campers forget to take clothing suitable for special activities. Once we participated in a camping trip to southern Missouri that included a

Quality raingear is very practical clothing for camping...

semi-formal dinner as part of the activities. Don remembered to pack a suit, a white shirt, black socks and a necktie for the occasion, but as he was dressing for the dinner, he realized his only footgear was a pair of ratty tennis shoes. A last-minute dash to a local shoe store resulted in the purchase of a pair of shoes that Don wore only that one evening because his feet require custom fittings.

Clothing for children should be packed that fit all occasions -- playing, fishing, social events, sightseeing, hiking, swimming, restaurants -- and for all weather, including rain, cold and hot temperatures and sometimes even snow. But, with two exceptions, we do not recommend purchasing any clothing especially for camping! Those two exceptions are raingear (ponchos or, preferably, rain suits) and footgear (shoes or boots and suitable socks) for hiking.

Unless your family is always flush with money (and

we don't know of any camping families that are!), buying kids' clothes just for camping is a waste of money. If you don't intend to go camping every week, the clothes probably will not be worn often enough to justify their purchase, and the kids are likely to outgrow everything within a year anyway. We have read magazine articles in which so-called experts recommended buying everything from color-coordinated outfits to kids' clothes made of special fabrics and shoes with certain kinds of soles. Frankly, doing that is stupid.

It is true that jeans are not among the best choices for camping clothes because they do not dry easily and can be too warm in the summer, but if your kids ordinarily wear nothing else but jeans, we do not suggest that you invest in cotton/canvas pants simply because they are regarded as more practical for camping. Similarly, if your kids like tee-shirts and sweatshirts, don't buy them flannels and special windbreakers.

NO FASHION STATEMENTS!

We strongly urge parents to take their kids camping with the types of clothes they would ordinarily wear around home. The purpose of a camping trip is personal enjoyment, and there is no need either to force your kids into wearing something they don't like simply to make a fashion statement or to do what someone else tells you is "correct." However, make sure enough clothes and shoes are packed so that a clean, dry outfit is always available.

If your budget can handle a few extra clothing items, we do recommend buying each kid a light, coated nylon jacket for use in various kinds of weather. Long underwear made of polypropylene is another good investment; it is lightweight, warm and dries quickly, and it is ideal for use

Hooded sweatshirts are good all-weather garments for camping kids...

in sleeping bags at night. Take at least two swimsuits for each youngster because wet swimsuits are uncomfortable and difficult to put on. Pack plenty of socks, in various styles, weights and fabrics. If your kids always wear pajamas at night, pack them; if they sleep in their underwear, that's okay for camping too. Layers of bedtime clothing are usually recommended for all campers, but our attitude is that the individual should sleep in what he regards as comfortable. We'll have to admit that our busy kids, as they were growing up, frequently slept in their clothes; sweatpants and sweatshirts frequently served double duty as daytime clothing and nighttime pajamas.

At least two pairs of shoes should be packed for every person because one pair will nearly always be either wet or muddy. We also suggest taking either slip-on shoes or those with Velcro fasteners for use if a nighttime walk is necessary. Pack gloves not only for warmth, but also for chopping wood, changing tires and doing other jobs around camp; RVers need a special pair of gloves for use in emptying holding tanks. We regard hooded sweatshirts as among the most versatile clothing that kids can take camping -- especially if the child dresses in layers of clothes, which we strongly recommend.

REMEMBER YOUR LIDS

Hats are quite important while camping. They keep heads warm, shade heads and eyes from the sun and provide valuable warmth at night when sleeping outside or in unheated tents. We always insist that each child take along a bright-colored hat that can be worn in crowds (such as at amusement parks). It is much easier to spot a bright purple hat at Disney World than it is to identify your child by his facial features.

Color-keying clothing as well as wash cloths and towels is useful when camping with several children. When we first started camping, we assigned specific colors to each of our kids and bought clothing and towels for them in those colors. After a short while, we stopped doing that with clothing, but we still assign towel colors to each family member.

We pack clothing such as socks, underwear and tee-shirts in zippered plastic bags to prevent them from floating from place to place on their own, and we used mesh bags (such as potato sacks) for carrying shoes and swimsuits. Do NOT take suitcases camping! They serve no worthwhile purpose and simply add to camp clutter.

EASILY FORGOTTEN ITEMS

Supplies and equipment that is not used by a family can be forgotten quite easily when packing for a camping trip. By the same token, very familiar items (such as pillows, towels and shoes) are often taken for granted, and those can be forgotten too. Our family always remembers to pack plenty of canned goods, but occasionally, we've forgotten to take a simple can opener. For families like ours that have automatic dishwashers at home, it's hard to remember dishwashing soap and dish towels. RV-campers also need to remember extra fuses for the trailer or motorhome, spare taillight bulbs, electric power supply adapter plugs, and a "Y" coupler for the water hose. Following a checklist should prevent important items from being left behind. Besides those just mentioned, here are items that we've discovered are easily forgotten unless special care is taken to pack them:

●Water purification tablets.

●Reading material, including books, magazines and crossword puzzles.

●Coffee pot.

●Trash bags.

●Work gloves.

●Polarized sunglasses.

●Binoculars.

●Life jackets.

●Cooking tongs, spatula and long-handled fork.

●Fire starter and wood matches.

●Knife sharpener.

●Folding chairs.

●RV toilet chemicals.

●Extra flashlight batteries and lantern mantles.

●Wire mesh holder for cooking hamburgers or fish over open fires.

●Toolbox.

●Spare shoelaces.

•Battery jumper cables.
•Lava soap, waterless hand cleaner and bath soap.
•Portable radio with batteries.

Toolboxes should include a flashlight, a Phillips-head and an RV-head screwdriver, a rag for wiping away grease, motor oil, a funnel, transmission fluid, windshield wiper fluid, Four-in-One oil, electrical tape, pliers and needle-nose pliers as well as tools that ordinarily would be stocked in every home toolbox.

PACKING YOUR GEAR

Unless your camping trip involves use of a rather large RV, space for storing all your food, clothing and gear is probably going to be at a premium. Options for increasing that space include a car-top carrier and storage pod or a rented utility trailer. Chances are, you will depend heavily upon the open area in the rear of your truck, van or car for packing most heavy items. If you do that and you are intending to tow a trailer or boat, you should be aware of one critical phenomenon of towing:

Hitches and vehicles are rated not only according to the trailer weights they can tow, but also according to the hitch weights they can handle. And contrary to popular belief, HITCH weights and trailer TONGUE weights are not the same thing. Hitch weight is the weight of the fully loaded towed vehicle's tongue PLUS the weight of the hitch itself AND the weight of everything that is loaded in the tow vehicle behind the rear axle. Therefore, when 250 pounds of gear are loaded into the trunk of a car towing a trailer with a 300-pound tongue weight, the combined rig's hitch weight is 550 pounds plus the weight of the hitch.

The primary importance of this fact is that it is quite easy to overload both a hitch and the rear of the tow vehicle. Obviously, an overloaded hitch can break. But what is not always recognized is that an overloaded tow vehicle is equally dangerous: Too much weight overloads the car's rear axle, suspension system, tires, wheels and brakes. In addition, placing too much weight in the rear of a car UNLOADS the vehicle's front axle and wheels and can make the car unmanageable to steer and more difficult to stop.

You can overload a car's rear end not only by putting too much gear in the trunk, but also by placing too much of it near the front of the trailer (remember, hitch weight includes the weight of the LOADED towed vehicle's tongue). On the other hand, if you pack too much stuff in the rear of a trailer, it can have two negative effects: unloading the trailer tongue, (making hitch weight too light for smooth towing) and overloading the rear of the trailer, resulting in what trailerists call tail-wag or sway.

PACK GEAR OVER THE AXLES

Common advice is to pack as much as possible over the axles of the towed vehicle. That is good advice unless you pack so much stuff that the axles are overloaded (every trailer has a gross axle rating, which is the amount of total weight the axles can carry).

Our advice: Don't endanger your family's lives by overpacking.

With that warning out of the way, let's concentrate on packing your gear for a trip. No matter what type of vehicles you are using in your travels, try to pack so that heavy weights are carried by the axles and the attitude of the vehicles remains as level to the ground as possible. Pack heavy items such as stacked cases of soft drinks in areas that are strongly reinforced. (A friend packed ten cases of Coke in an RV closet, only to discover while traveling that the floor of the closet was not built to handle that much weight. The floor collapsed.)

Here are some packing tips you might find valuable:

Items that are seldom used and those that will be used in the future should be packed first and placed in the hard-to-reach spaces such as in floor-level nooks and crannies of an RV, under an RV's bench dinette seats and under a bed or sofa.

Designate specific areas of the RV (or car or van) in which each child can store his clothing and his personal possessions.

Specify an easy-to-reach place where spare shoes are to be kept at all times.

Store as much as possible in layers, keeping similar items (trousers, tee-shirts, canned goods, etc.) together.

Tools, outdoor cooking equipment, lawn chairs and other items not necessary to the function of an RV's interior should be kept in outside storage compartments.

Try to store each person's towels and wash cloths (which we color-assign to family members) in the same place every time.

Let the kids pack their own supplies and clothes, but check the results (taking care not to insult them by "inspecting" their work).

Place games, puzzles, coloring books and similar items so they can be unpacked easily for use while traveling.

Pack a surprise gift for each kid that can be opened during a rainy day.

Once all the packing is done and preparations are made for your camping trip, it is time for one final decision: When will you depart on vacation?

Chapter 10

When to Leave Home

The main difference between then and now was that we were a lot younger then than we are now. Of course, our kids were a lot smaller then, but that wasn't the primary reason we were able to leave home on weekend camping trips in the middle of the night on Friday and return during the early evening hours on Sunday after we'd traveled 300 miles each way and jammed in a weekend of camping, fishing, swimming, boating, sightseeing and shopping!

We camped seven hours from home on the shore of Lake Cumberland without benefit of modern facilities -- not even a restroom -- and without the companionship or safety provided by other campers. We had no money. Not even enough for a real campsite across the bay at the small state-owned landing, where sites were only $3 a night and the restrooms were pit toilets. Not enough for a lunch on the way at McDonald's. Our only pleasures were what we did with each other, but we enjoyed ourselves immensely.

Given the opportunity, would we do it over again? Absolutely! But would we travel and camp that way now? Not a chance!

If you are a young parent reading this, we realize that even if we give you our best advice on when to leave home on your family camping trip, you probably won't do it as we suggest; you'll do it when we did it -- at the first opportunity. That probably means you'll launch your trip on Friday night after the parental work week ends. Or, maybe you'll even take off work on Friday and leave early -- not on Friday morning, but on Thursday evening.

It could be that you'll pack your camping rig fully on Friday with the intention of hitting the road Saturday morning after breakfast. But chances are good that one of you will awaken on Friday in the middle of the night and say, "If we left now, we could get an early jump on the weekend traffic..." and by the time the sun rises over the horizon, you will have already logged a hundred miles or so on the way to your camping destination.

WHAT YOU OUGHT TO DO
Okay. So here's what we suggest: Get a good night's sleep and begin the first day of your camping vacation well rested. Eat a light but nutritious breakfast. Plan periodic rest stops along the route so that one person does not drive more than three or four hours at a stretch. Take your time and drive well within the speed limit. Allow plenty of time for a mid-day meal. Plan to arrive at a campground a few hours before dark so that you can set up camp leisurely and enjoy some quiet time with your family before going to bed.

That's not the way we always began our family camping trips, but it's the way we begin them now that our kids are grown.

Since we're confident that you won't follow our advice, let us offer you a few tips instead.

Don't wait until you are ready to leave before you finish packing. Load as many supplies as possible in your camping rig as far in advance of your trip as you can because you probably will leave home on the spur of the moment, and doing that will increase the likelihood that you'll forget to pack something. This is an excellent time to pack your childrens' toys, books and games.

Don't plan a heavy work schedule on the day before you plan to leave. If you decide to leave earlier, you don't need to cope with the stress of trying to jam a full day of business into a few hours of schedule-shifting.

GET THE KIDS READY TO GO
On the night before launch day, dress the kids in sleeping gear that is warm and comfortable and something they can wear in the car if you decide to carry them out of the house in the middle of the night. Be sure to stock the vacation vehicle with enough blankets and pillows for them.

After leaving 28 hours ahead of schedule in the middle of the night on the day before your vacation was supposed to start, plan to stop for a family breakfast sometime after dawn when the kids begin to awaken. Stopping will allow you to unwind, and it will provide the kids with an opportunity to get out of their pajamas.

Do not, under any circumstances, take a briefcase loaded with work from the office. You won't ever get around to doing the work anyway, so why clutter up your vacation vehicle with it?

There are several advantages to driving all night in

order to reach your camping destination, but one big plus is that when the kids awaken early in the morning and ask that age-old question, "Are we there yet?" you can honestly answer, "We'll be there in about ten minutes."

Chapter 11

Campsite Reservations

For nearly 30 years, we have been hit with a constant barrage of appeals that we and other camping families should always make campsite reservations while we are traveling or vacationing. The appeals, of course, come from the campground industry. Indeed, there are good reasons for making reservations, but what the campground industry always ignores is that there are also good reasons for not making them. One of our biggest criticisms of campground operators is that they have initiated policies that actually discourage families from making reservations. We'll explain that statement a little later, but first, let's look at the good reasons for making reservations.

The most obvious reason for reservations is that they ensure you will have a campsite which fits your needs when you arrive at your destination. A family that enjoys stopping at a campsite it has visited before probably should always make reservations so there is no chance of being disappointed by a lack of spaces at the time of arrival. Don't ever assume that your favorite campground will not be full at the time you intend to visit it; construction work, facilities problems, an RV club rally or a special event that you know nothing about could seriously change the number of open sites available.

In addition, calling ahead for reservations provides you with the opportunity to learn about such unexpected developments. After being told that the campground will host a large RV rally at the time you intend to be there, you might decide to camp somewhere else in order to avoid a crowd. If you particularly enjoy camping at a specific site in your favorite park, you should call ahead so that site will be reserved for you.

WHEN KEEPING TO A SCHEDULE

Some individuals travel best when they are following a specific schedule. They want to know where they will be at all times. The reasons for that varies: the need for a sense of security; they want to follow a travel itinerary so friends or family members can reach them in an emergency, or they simply function best when they can pre-plan each stage of their trip.

Campsite reservations can certainly prevent families from worrying about whether all the sites will be gone when they arrive at their destination, and especially for some children, avoiding that stress is important. When Don was a boy, his family took him on a camping trip to northern Minnesota. As the family traveled northward from their home in Ohio, Don became concerned by the large volume of traffic that was traveling in the same direction. He noticed that many of the other travelers carried camping equipment and towed boats, and he was worried that they might be going to the same destination and filling the area with crowds of people. As the trip progressed and camper/ boater traffic continued to be heavy, Don became more and more concerned until he finally expressed his worries to his parents. They calmed his fears by explaining not only that their campsite was reserved, but also that virtually all of the other travelers had different destinations.

Camping friends of ours have told us they experience almost unbearable stress if they are faced with searching for a campground at the end of a long day. For them, daily reservations are extremely important. Some campers even find it stressful to look for a suitable campsite within a campground; reservations can prevent that stress by allowing a specific site to be assigned in advance.

POPULAR TOURIST AREAS

During seasons when camping traffic is high in some areas, reservations might be unavoidable. Campgrounds in and around Yellowstone National Park, for example, are often reserved for weeks in advance during the peak summer tourist period. Disney World's Fort Wilderness campground is so heavily booked that reservations of several months in advance are required for some time periods. At times, advance registrations also are necessary in order to camp in areas of Florida, south Texas, around Myrtle Beach and in some national parks.

Unless our family intends to stop at a major tourist area for a specific amount of time, we never make reservations, however. There are two primary reasons we do not like to make campground reservations:

ONE -- Our travel plans change frequently and suddenly, and we insist upon having complete freedom over where and when we will travel. We feel campsite reservations lock us into a rigid travel schedule that reduces our freedom of movement and our sense of adventure.

TWO -- Making and breaking reservations can be expensive. Frequently, reservation charges are added to the campsite fee. We resent paying those reservations charges, and we resent it even more if we pay the charges and then change our travel plans. Also, many campgrounds insist upon charging families for days that campsites are reserved even if the family's travel plans change. Our resentment of such policies knows no bounds, and we refuse to patronize campgrounds that require reservations and will not give refunds.

COSTLY CHANGE OF PLANS

A couple of years ago, we reserved a campsite for a week in a wilderness section of northern Minnesota not far from the Boundary Waters Canoe Area. It was a beautiful, scenic site on an excellent fishing lake, and the property owner operated a nearby lodge where good food was served. It seemed like an ideal location for us when we checked it out, and we were convinced we would spend a week there. During the next few days, however, the wanderlust hit us and we decided to leave a couple of days early. Because we were the only campers occupying a site, it was clear to us that demand for the campground's space was not a pressing issue, so we did not expect an argument when we told the property owner about our change in plans.

He amazed us by insisting that we pay him for the entire week. We tried pointing out that our occupation of the site had not discouraged other campers because there weren't any other campers! However, he demanded payment anyway, claiming successful operation of the campground depended upon being able to anticipate a specific amount of income week by week. That argument seemed ludicrous to us because if we had not told him we were going to camp on his site for a week, we could have camped there day by day without being concerned about when we left. And, we emphasized, he had not given us a reduced rate for committing to the site for a week; we paid the same rate as overnight campers. Again, he rejected our points and said if we had decided to camp there one day at a time, he would have reserved the right to assign us to another site in the event a week-long camping party arrived.

In the end, we paid the man for a full week of camping, but in spite of the fact that we liked camping there, we informed him we would never return and would recommend to our friends that they not camp there either. Later, we speculated among ourselves that his fee policies might have been responsible for the decisions of other families not to camp there, resulting in the poor demand for his sites.

PRECEDENT IS THERE

It is a common practice for air and automobile travelers to make reservations at hotels and motels without facing financial penalties if plans change. Room reservations made for more than a few days, and even a week or two, can be scaled back to fit the traveler's circumstances. So long as reservations are canceled in time for a room to be rented to someone else, hotel operators do not even consider charging for it. Frequently, even last-minute cancelations made too late to benefit the hotel are permitted.

Many campground operators, however, insist that site fees be paid for every night of a reservation, no matter what the circumstances. That policy absolutely destroys the sense of freedom which is an important focal point of the camping lifestyle.

As a consequence, our family would rather take our chances on finding a satisfactory overnight camping space than make reservations at a campground and be forced to pay for a site we do not use if our plans change. We like to take side trips and make impulsive stops at interesting attractions as we travel. The freedom to do that is important to us because it lends to our quest for adventure. If we wanted to follow a rigid vacation schedule, we would travel by airplanes and sleep overnight in motels, not travel/camp our way across the country!

Side trips and frequent stops can change a day's travel schedule by several hours and make it impossible to arrive at an original destination on time. Searching for another campground along our route becomes necessary. Quite often, our kids enjoy some aspect of the side trip so much that they request to spend more time there; that means we must find a campground nearby and delay arrival at the destination for an even longer period. Not having reservations anywhere for any specific periods permits those kinds of travel schedule adjustments.

A SENSE OF ADVENTURE

We should add that we truly enjoy searching out new places to camp, however, and the uncertainty of what types of camping facilities are available at parks we've never visited only adds to our sense of adventure. In all the years we have camped, we have never been turned away from a campground because it was full. Admittedly, on a few occasions we have had to camp in an overflow area, but quite often, those sections are more scenic and quieter than a campground's primary sites.

Campground personnel nearly always are very helpful to new visitors and welcome the opportunity to suggest nearby places for families to enjoy themselves. Our kids have had so much fun during a few of these side trips that we have changed a whole month or two of travel plans in order to spend more time in a locale that we did not initially intend to visit!

There are two times when we do make advance revations. One is if we plan to visit a popular tourist area or a heavily used campground and want to make sure a space is available. The other time is when we're traveling in an RV caravan with several other families. For caravan groups, reservations are necessary in order for individual families to break away on their own but still know where they can rejoin the group. Also, quite often a campground operator will give special attention to a caravan group, either setting aside a section of the park for them or even planning special events for them.

Several years ago we were part of a caravan by families of RV company executives from northern Indiana to the popular tourist town of Frankenmuth, Michigan. There were about 30 individuals in our group, including a dozen children. The owner of the Frankenmuth Campground, an excellent businessman who is quite active in his industry's state and national organizations, provided us with attention that went way beyond what might be expected. He permitted one member of our party to register the whole group, he parked us together in a convenient section of the park near the playground, an activities area and an enclosed shelter, and he prepared a large campfire for us to use that evening. When we told him we wanted to eat dinner at the Bavarian Inn -- a world-famous Frankenmuth restaurant that does not take reservations -- he telephoned the owner of that establishment and arranged for us to avoid long lines by making a privately escorted entrance to tables that were prepared especially for us.

Chapter 12

Count Heads

During the summer of 1975, our family combined a business trip with a camping vacation and traveled from our home in Ohio to the Smoky Mountains of North Carolina. It was a tightly scheduled trip because Don had arranged interviews with several different people in order to research a series of magazine articles. There was no spare time between interviews for sightseeing or side trips because there was just barely enough time for us to drive our mini-motorhome from one interview to the next.

Because our little motorhome had no bathroom, we were forced to make frequent pit stops to accommodate our four small children. Each stop, of course, affected our schedule and forced us to drive faster in order to make up time and meet our appointments. One particularly frustrating stop occurred in Tennessee when we halted for gasoline and all four kids left the motorhome to explore, buy refreshments and go to the restrooms. They were bored and restless and required shouts and threats of bodily harm before they returned to their seats.

Later, as we sped through the mountains on a two-lane highway, we were surprised when a crazy motorist started to pass us on a curve and then drove alongside us for a short distance before finally speeding around our motorhome. As the car passed, we saw our four-year-old son Micah grinning and waving at us out its rear window! We had neglected to count heads when we left the service station earlier and had left Micah behind in the restroom. Fortunately, a family traveling our direction had volunteered to chase us down.

Since then, we've always counted heads to make sure all our kids were present *before* leaving anyplace.

WELL, NOT EXACTLY *ALWAYS*

Correction. We've *almost* always counted heads. About a year after the incident in Tennessee, we left Micah standing alone at the exit to the Kings Island amusement park while we boarded trams and returned to our car. Fortunately, we remembered him before we left the parking lot.

Loving our kids as much as we do, we once wondered if we were watching out for them too casually. But we've heard dozens of similar stories about traveling parents who have left children behind and we've come to realize that what we did was not unusual.

Even so, we have tried to take special precautions to prevent our children from becoming lost or separated from us. For us, there has always been somewhat of an emotional conflict between protecting our kids and giving them the amount of independence they deserve. And counting heads is just not enough!

During our travels, we try to make sure we know

where our kids are at all times. There are degrees to that knowledge, however. When our kids were small, we wanted to know *exactly* where they were, what they were doing and who they were with. As they grew older, we were satisfied with knowing *approximately* where they were (and sub-consciously, we probably didn't always want to know what they were doing or who they were doing it with).

Even now, with our two youngest kids nearing adulthood, we expect to be told when they leave the campsite, where they are going and when they expect to return.

When we visited attractions that were crowded with tourists -- for example, amusement parks -- we insisted that each of our kids wear bright-colored shirts and hats so that we could spot them easily. Doing that has helped us keep track of them, but it certainly did not prevent us from leaving Micah behind at Kings Island.

None of our children ever got lost while camping, but we know that happens, and it must be a terrible experience for both parents and the child. Two of the precautions we took when camping or hiking in the wilderness were to provide each child with a compass (and show him how to use it) and to give each kid a whistle that he could blow if he became separated from us. Each parent also carried a whistle on those occasions, and we'll admit we used ours a great deal more frequently than the kids used theirs.

Chapter 13

Games On the Road

There is no known way to prevent children from becoming bored while they are traveling for long periods of time. Our best hope when we took our kids camping was that we could reduce their periods of boredom to brief intervals sandwiched among attractions, meals, sightseeing, books, naps and games. We learned very early in our camping years not to depend upon beautiful scenery to help relieve kids' boredom; for them, if you've seen one mountain or river, you've seen them all!

There is no question that parents should do all they can to prevent boredom, however. When kids travel together, boredom inevitably leads to arguments, arguments lead to fights, and fights can create havoc with a family vacation.

Games are the parents' secret weapons in their constant war with boredom. But those weapons have to be stockpiled selectively, and the parent must be armed with a good variety of them in order to have an effective offense.

A reality of family life is that kids become bored with games almost as easily as they are bored by scenery, so parents have to be ready to switch strategies and games at the first hint of a yawn.

To make some of the games more appealing, parents can take along several prizes -- either silly ones or useful ones -- that can be awarded to winners of some of the games. To make competition for those prizes fair among different age groups of children, older children can be assigned handicaps based on their ages.

Our recommended games armory includes imagination games, board games, sports, nature games, crafts and educational or learning games. Unfortunately, unless you are traveling in an motorhome, board games and crafts are not of much value while on the road. Even so-called "travel" versions of popular board games do not work well in the back seat of a crowded automobile. Sports activities and most nature games are limited to rest areas and campgrounds. So that means an on-the-road arsenal of games for most traveling families has to be limited to those emphasizing imagination and learning.

IMAGINATION GAMES

Imagination games are among the best travel games to play with older children because they stimulate the kids intellectually and stir their creative juices. The most common type of imagination game is story-telling. In its simplest form, it requires only that the story-teller be offered a a topic, and it is the story-teller's responsibility to tell the most interesting story he can create from his imagination. This game can be modified into a contest quite easily by allowing each child to tell a story for a limited amount of time -- one or two minutes, for example. After every child has had a turn, all the listeners vote on the best story.

Another version of this game is for the first child to be given a story topic; before the child can speak on that topic very long, he is stopped and another child is assigned to take up the story from that point. The shortcoming of this type of game is that children tend to lose interest in it rather quickly. The major value of it is that it is a good way for older children to entertain younger kids, who are usually quite amused by the silly progress of the story.

LAUGHING IN THE AISLES

If your children are especially imaginative, they can try to entertain each other by telling jokes or creating stand-up comedy routines. Our son Thad fancied himself as an excellent joke-teller when he was 6-8 years old, and he constantly tried to entertain the rest of us with jokes that he created as he was telling them. Nearly always, they were terrible and corny, but sometimes they were quite funny.

A favorite traveling game of our children was the "I went to the store" game. The object of this game was for the kids to work their way through the alphabet one letter at a time by announcing what they bought at the store, including each of the items mentioned earlier. For example, the first child would say, "I went to the store and bought an apple." The second would say, "I went to the store and bought an apple and a banana." The third bought an apple, a banana and a carrot, and so on until every letter in the alphabet was covered. If anyone could not think of an appropriate purchase, or if he forgot one of the earlier items, he was disqualified. A more difficult version of this game was to mention items bought, but not relate them to the alphabet. Our children seldom finished this game before losing interest in it, but it would keep them occupied for 10 or 15 minutes each time they played it.

Our children created a game of their own that they enjoyed playing endlessly but which did not make much sense to us, their parents. Here's how it went: Each one in turn would count off three cars that were traveling on the highway in the opposite direction, and the fourth vehicle would become "his" car. A Mercedes or a sports car would earn cheers, but an old junker sedan or school bus would encourage the other kids to ridicule "his" vehicle. The game was punctuated by comments such as "Hey Dad, Chris got a dump truck, but I got a Rolls Royce!"

The most popular game our children played while traveling -- and one that they usually convinced Mom and Dad to play too -- was called "I see see." One player would announce, "I see see something that begins with the letter 'T,'" and the other family members would try to guess the item. Rules were that the item he identified had to be within everyone's viewing and if, for some reason, the item was no longer visible either inside or outside the car, he was required to say so. Our children became quite creative with this game by selecting items by names other than the ones they were ordinarily called. For example, the "T" item might be a "twig" and not the "Tree" that was certain to be identified quickly. Or a "B" item might be the "bark" of a tree. If family members were unable to identify the item selected, the same child would get another turn. Anyone who identified the item, however, took over control of the game and selected a new item.

LEARNING GAMES

Another game that was almost as popular involved everyone in the family, teamed according to where they sat in the vehicle. Those on the driver's side played as a team against those on the co-pilot's side. The goal of each team was to find objects or words on signs that began with each letter of the alphabet, in order. Thus, the team on the driver's side looked for objects and words on that side of the road while the team on the co-pilot's side tried to see objects and words on that side. The letters "q" and "x" did not have to be spotted. Concepts or ideas such as "agriculture" were not permitted. Thad and Don tended to dominate this game, so a standing family rule was that they were not allowed to play on the same team.

Some of the games our kids played required a referee, and Pam was almost always assigned to that job. One game involved her announcing the name of a state, and the child who identified its capitol was declared the winner.

NAME THE CITIES

A similar game which was often played by the children of another couple we knew was an alphabet-type contest in which either state or city names were identified in order of the alphabet. If the city "Albuquerque" were selected to represent "A," the child who selected it was also required to tell, correctly, the name of the city's state. A child correctly identifying an "A" city or state would have the opportunity to assign "B" to a city or state and move through the alphabet until he either made an incorrect assignment or was unable to make a selection. When that happened, the first child making a correct selection could continue through the alphabet. A second version of this game would allow the new turn to begin with the letter "A," but cities and towns identified earlier were not eligible to be identified again. Using this second version, each player's score would be kept, and the child with the highest score either at the end of a time limit or after all alphabet

letters were correctly assigned would be declared the winner.

Another state capitol game is one in which each
contestant is given a sheet of paper listing names of the 50
states. Players are asked to write the appropriate state capitols beside each of the state names, and the one who identifies the most capitols within a time limit is declared the
winner. A modified version of this allows the children to
use a second list with the capitols named in alphabetical
order. They must match the capitol names with the correct
states.

A very educational game, but one that is too difficult
for most children to play, involves naming each state's
nickname, motto, flower, tree, bird and song. We suspect
that several different versions of this game could be created. Hint: Answers to each of these categories are included
in the state-by-state listings of our two popular books,
Guide to Free Attractions and *Save-A-Buck Camping*.

A game that involves numbers and counting can be
played for the entire duration of a trip and include all members of the family who are able to count into the hundreds.
The rules are simple: Each person is required to see succes-
sive numbers on signs, billboards or license plates. Only
full numbers qualify, not a small number within a larger
one. And only one player (or a team of players) is permitted to claim each number. The winning player or team is
the one claiming the largest number after a specified time
limit or when the family arrives at its destination.

Another good team game is played by assigning numbers to various types of animals. A cow is worth 1 point; a
horse, 2 points; a sheep, 3 points; a pig, 1 point; a cat, 1
point; a dog, 2 points; a chicken, 1 point; a goat, 3 points;
a hawk, 5 points; a fox, 10 points; an eagle; 20 points; a

deer, 7 points. Each group of animals spotted is considered as a single animal. Points are awarded when a team member spots the qualifying animals on the team's side of the road. If a church steeple is seen, the team's points double. If a member of the opposite team spots a cemetery on the opposing team's side of the road, the opposing team's point total is reduced to zero. Qualifying animals can be added according to the part of the country the family travels through.

WHICH RV IS IT?

Children who are veteran travelers and RVers could play a game that tests their RV-recognition skills. Each time an RV is seen approaching from the opposite direction, players guess its brand. The player who guesses 10 RV brands first is the winner. Our kids became quite good at identifying RVs from long distances by nothing more than their front profiles.

Carousel Press, which produces the "Family Travel Guides" book catalogs, has created a good, relatively noise-free educational game called the United States License Plate Game. Using a basic U.S. map with states outlined and identified by name, players try to spot license plates from the various states. Each time a player identifies a plate from a new state, he colors in the state with either a crayon or a felt-tipped pen. Obviously, the winner will have the most colorful map at the end of the contest.

As the license plate game is played, the child can cross-check state locations using the Rand McNally road atlas that you bought for him (you did remember to bring it along, didn't you?). Using the atlas to follow the family's route also will keep a kid entertained for very brief periods during the trip, but it has other values too. If your family

has copies of our free-attractions guide and our free-camp-grounds directories, older children can use those in conjunction with the atlas to keep tabs on interesting places to stop along the route

OTHER GAMES

One type of packaged game that our children enjoyed playing, even under rather crowded seating conditions, was Yahtzee. This popular dice game requires a flat surface on which the dice can be rolled, but otherwise, it is quite easy to play while traveling. When vacationing in a motorhome or a van equipped with a stationary table, travel versions of the Scrabble, Bingo and Cribbage games can be played.

Of course, card games of all kinds are fun to play while traveling in a motorhome or van. Our kids have been fanatic card-players since they were small children, and new decks of cards are always listed on our supplies list as items to be restocked periodically. During one period when all three of our sons were teenagers, they and Don played penny-ante poker for ten hours at the motorhome dinette while Pam drove from our home in Indiana to our destination in Omaha. It takes real card fanatics to do that!

Small children and babies are relatively easy to entertain while traveling, but the key to preventing them from being bored is to pay attention to them almost constantly. Keeping youngsters occupied was always a shared responsibility in our family, and our older kids were quite good at playing with the smaller ones for long periods of time, especially when we traveled in a motorhome. Small children like being cuddled as much as possible, even by older siblings, and that can be combined with reading picture-books to them, telling them stories or singing songs.

Coloring books and felt-tipped pens (crayons melt when left inside a vehicle on hot summer days) are good ways to keep small children occupied. Our kids also enjoyed books of crossword puzzles, connect-the-dots and similar puzzles as they got older. Sarah, who is 18 years old as this is being written, still takes crossword puzzle books with her wherever she travels.

CAMPSITE GAMES

Games and planned activities can be important diversions for kids even after your family has arrived at your camping destination. Although most campgrounds today offer a wide variety of events to keep kids occupied, there are times when no events are scheduled, or the weather interferes with those that were planned, and the children feel they don't have anything to do. Those rare occasions are when enterprising parents should pull activities out of their arsenal.

If the weather permits, physical activities are the best way to relieve kids' boredom and work off excess energy. Games that you would not suggest at home can be initiated at a campground and enjoyed as rare privileges. Examples: water balloon tosses, water pistol fights, pie-eating contests. Both Mom and Dad can participate in those activities too, especially since kids enjoy few things more than dousing their parents with water or seeing Dad with berry pie all over his face.

NEVER TOO YOUNG

One summer when we were camped in Minnesota, Don and our two oldest sons had a water fight, and the boys joined forces to soak their father from head to foot. He retaliated by dragging the two of them to a campsite faucet and putting their heads under the water. It was great fun for the three of them, but as they grabbed towels and dry clothes and walked toward the bathhouse, Don was surprised to be hit with a pail of water from behind. He turned around, and there stood our smallest son, three-year-old Micah, who grinned and asked, "Are you gonna put my head under the faucet too?" Of course, Don did, accompanied by Micah's delighted squeals, and then the four of them hiked to the bathhouse.

Activities such as pitching horseshoes (many campgrounds have pits and shoes), tossing a baseball or playing other games outdoors also are good diversions for camping kids. There are many other less obvious activities that are equally good, however. Here are some suggestions:

•Hold a scavenger hunt of items usually found in and around a campground.

•Begin a leaf, rock, shell, pinecone or beach treasure

collection.

•Make wind chimes from shells, hollow pieces of wood, and other pieces of natural debris strung on fishing line.

•Catch fireflies.

•Organize a treasure hunt for buried treasure (using clues that one of the older children created for his camping project).

•Take a nature hike or an afternoon backpacking trip on the campground's hiking trails.

•Organize a picnic.

•Rent bicycles for a family ride.

•Go horseback riding if there is a stable nearby that rents horses.

YOU'RE BUILDING MEMORIES

No matter which activities you choose, do your best to select those which the kids ordinarily would not take part in at home. You will be surprised how long the memories of those camping activities will be remembered by you and the children during the years ahead.

Before closing this chapter, we'd like to mention an interesting phenomenon about our kids and their travel habits. From the time they were quite small, whenever we left home on a camping trip, they would almost instantly fall asleep. Sometimes, they would be asleep before we were a mile from our house! We have never met any other families whose children did that, but we think we know why ours did. As we mentioned earlier in this book, most of our early camping trips started in the middle of the night when we carried our pajama-clad youngsters to our little mini-motorhome and then drove for several hours to our weekend destinations. We believe our kids became so acclimated to sleeping while traveling, and then awakening to enjoy a wide range of outdoor activities, that going to sleep as they left home became part of their camping routine.

Chapter 14

The First
Night in Camp

Unless you are familiar with the campground where you are going to vacation, we recommend against reserving a specific campsite in advance of your arrival. The site where your family will spend several days, a couple of weeks or even longer should meet your specific needs and provide you with the best possible camping environment. Even if a campground employee assigns a specific site to you when you arrive, the ultimate decision of where you camp is yours, not the employee's. That is an unspoken stipulation between campers and campground operators.

In most cases, when you register for a campsite, a campground employee will automatically select a site for you unless you request to select your own. Most experienced campground operators will ask you a brief series of questions before assigning you a site so that they can place you in an area and on a site that they believe will satisfy you. Their questions will relate to the size of your family, the ages of your children, the type of camping rig you have, the length of your vehicles and the types of services or facilities you particularly want. In most cases, you can trust an experienced campground employee to choose a satisfactory site for you. But, occasionally, you will not agree with that choice.

Quite often, the operator of a sparsely populated campground will not even assign a site to you. He will either tell you to select any site you like, or he will recommend a particular area of the park to you and suggest you make a selection from that area. Occasionally, you will select the wrong site for yourself.

Accepted practice is for you to drive to an assigned site and examine it. If you do not like it or think it is unsuitable for one reason or another, identify another site that you like better, then go back to the campground office and ask for that site. Campground operators are almost always very nice, courteous and cooperative. Like any other business people, they do not want dissatisfied customers, so they probably will reassign you to the site you want without any argument. Once in a while, they will give you a reason you weren't assigned to that site originally -- perhaps it is reserved for a regular customer, or maybe it has a water drainage problem that is not obvious. In all the years we have camped, we have never met a campground operator who was not willing to assign us to a site other than the one that was first selected for us.

Obviously, the site selected should be as level as possible. Erecting a tent or setting up an RV on an off-level site is inconvenient at best, and sometimes, it can prove to be quite unpleasant. Tent-campers need to make sure the site also has good surface drainage and is not likely to be flooded in the event of rain. For RV-campers, a pull-through site is convenient to use when overnight camping, but is less important for long-term stops unless you are camped in a motorhome that must be used as transportation every time you leave the campground.

When inspecting the site, make sure utility connections are placed conveniently for your use. If you are camped in an RV that has a sewer outlet at mid-coach, you do not want a site with its sewer connection located 15 feet away from your outlet. Watch for overhanging tree limbs and make sure you can park under them without damaging your rig. One consideration of critical importance when camping with kids is the type of environment around the site. Is it clean, muddy, sandy? Is it likely to become quite muddy in rainy weather? Is the dirt or sand the kind that will be tracked into your tent or RV too easily? Look for anthills (particularly fire ants in the South) and evidence of other insects. Make sure the site is upwind from its campfire ring; you don't want the inside of your tent or RV to smell like smoke.

LOCATION, LOCATION, LOCATION

When tent-camping, try to select a site that allows the tent to face southeast so that it will be warmed by the morning sun. The availability of shade in the afternoon should be considered too.

The site's location within the campground also can be very important to you. If your family intends to use the bathhouse, is the site close enough for a short nighttime trek? Consider the site's location to the swimming pool, playground, game room and laundry if those services and features are desirable to you. Keep in mind that while a site alongside the park pool might seem to be convenient, you will have to accept the noise that goes along with having the pool nearby. A site that is ten feet from the shower rooms might seem to be a good one for you until you consider whether a couple of banging bathhouse doors will keep you awake all night.

In some areas of the country, the most rustic and scenic sites might not be appropriate for family camping. Don particularly recalls one of his first RV-camping trips with his father in the early 1960s. When they arrived at the northern Minnesota campground on a hot but windy summer day, they were amazed to see that all the other campers were parked in the middle of the campground on open, unshaded sites. All the most beautiful, scenic sites under large stands of trees were not being used. Almost gloating with pleasure over this discovery, they immediately parked under a huge elm tree on a site that was well screened and protected from the wind by evergreens and young pines.

SCENIC ISN'T EVERYTHING

Moments after they began setting up camp, they discovered why the other campers had avoided such a perfect setting: Swarms of mosquitoes attacked them from all directions. The mosquitoes, they learned later, nested in the cool environment under and in the trees, unhampered by bright sunlight and the wind. Convinced they would be able to deal with the huge population of mosquitoes, Don and his father finished setting up camp and spent their first night swatting insects that found ways to fly inside the small travel trailer. Then early the next morning, before other campers awakened to take notice of what they were doing, they quietly moved to another site in the middle of the campground.

Chapter 15

Building a Campfire

Campfires are a tradition in our family, and after you build one and enjoy it while camping with your kids, we'll bet they become traditional with your family too. The value of campfires is the romance and nostalgia they provide, not the light at night, not the fire for cooking food, and not even the warmth. Camping is supposed to be a primitive form of travel and recreation; everything kids read and hear about camping tells them that. And to live primitively, even if it is warm and snug inside a $200,000 motorhome, one has to have a campfire!

We built a campfire the first time we took our kids camping, and we've built one nearly every time since then. When our kids were younger and they all traveled with us, we could not even consider camping without a campfire. They enjoyed cooking hotdogs and roasting marshmallows over its flames, and they liked to relax around it at night, but they relished the sense of security and belonging that it provided them more than they appreciated its functional value.

Among their best memories of camping as they were growing up were the evenings spent around campfires.

For kids, an important part of the campfire experience is actually building the fire. Recognizing that, we gave the campfire-starting duties to our children as soon as they were old enough to handle matches safely. First, of course, we taught them how to do it -- always using natural materials collected from around the campground. And, based on our experiences with teaching our children to build a fire, here is the procedure we recommend to you:

ONE -- Gather an ample supply of firewood, preferably using wood provided by or purchased from the campground operator or park ranger. Good, seasoned firewood can be collected from nearby wooded areas if it is available, but make certain doing that is permissible, and do not collect green wood or damage standing trees. To burn properly, firewood should be cut into pieces about 18 inches long and split, but doing that is not absolutely necessary.

TWO -- After a couple of armloads of firewood has been collected and stacked near the fire pit, select various types of starter material. Dried grass, small twigs from dead branches, and dry leaves are excellent starters, and it can be supplemented with paper if necessary. If none of that material is available, shave some thin strips of wood from the firewood logs. Then gather slightly larger pieces of wood (large twigs and small branches are satisfactory) for kindling.

THREE -- Build a small, very loose nest of the grass, leaves, paper and twigs in the middle of the fire pit, and stack the smallest pieces of kindling around it in a tepee shape. Make sure to leave open space for air flow, but it might be necessary to shelter the nest from wind until the fire is burning fully.

FOUR -- Light one or two corners of the next with a

a wood kitchen match or some other safe fire-starting tool. It might be necessary to blow on the fire softly in order to keep the tiny embers glowing until flames ignite the starter. Rearrange the tepee'd kindling if necessary so that the flames take hold, and once the kindling is burning, add a few small pieces of firewood until the flames move from the kindling to the larger logs. Be careful not to smother the fire by putting on too much wood and cutting off its air circulation.

FIVE -- After the split firewood is burning brightly with strong flames, large logs can be put into the fire.

A fire should never be allowed to die and go out on its own; it should be put out with water and then the coals smothered by covering them with sand or dirt. Children old enough to build a fire should be given responsibility for extinguishing it after they are taught how to do it properly. They should learn that part of the responsibility for starting a campfire is putting it out; we believe if they learn that, extinguishing fires will become second nature to them as they grow into adults and take their own children camping.

Usually, we set a campfire hour which all members of the family are expected to attend. Traditionally, that period starts just after dark, but sometimes the kids are so impatient to enjoy their campfire that they insist upon beginning before dusk. At a typical campfire hour, we cook hotdogs, marshmallows and s'mores (which are chocolate bars and marshmallows sandwiched between graham crackers and heated over the fire in a long-handled pie iron). Some time is spent discussing events of the day and making plans for tomorrow, but the campfire hour also is a good excuse for the kids to snuggle close to Mom and Dad and be cuddled.

No matter what the campfire activities are, however,

the kids are always the primary focus. It is their fire and their special time.

Chapter 16

Photography

During the many years we wrote camping and travel articles for magazines, all our camping trips were thoroughly documented on film because we needed color photographs to illustrate the articles. Today, we have a wealth of family pictures beyond belief, including photos of our kids as they grew up camping, having fun and sightseeing in nearly every section of North America. We did not shoot the pictures in order to record our trips and preserve our experiences, but if our intention had been to do that, we would have produced the same kinds of photos that we shot for the magazines.

Think about this: The purpose of taking cameras on a camping trip is to create a permanent photographic record of the trip, the places visited and the experiences.

If you keep those goals in mind and convey them to your kids when they pack their cameras for your family camping vacation, the resulting photographs are likely to include a collection of photos that will give you and the

Photograph family members to illustrate the story of your trip...

kids many hours of pleasure during the future. Approach the trip as if it were a professional photographic assignment; shoot a wide variety of pictures -- people, places, scenery and action -- from several different angles and distances. And capture all the moments you can on film!

Earlier, we recommended that each child who wants

to take a camera should be provided with one. The new automatic 35-mm cameras are relatively inexpensive, and they provide excellent color photos and slides. We also suggested buying bulk quantities of film, in 36-exposure rolls, to save money, and we recommended buying considerably more film than you expect to need, partly because your family will use more of it than you expect, and the left-over film will be used around home after the trip ends.

We suggest purchasing two different speeds of film. (A film's speed is its measurable sensitivity to light; the higher the ASA speed number, the less light is needed for a good picture.) For good, all-around pictures outdoors on bright, sunny days, choose 100-speed color film. Approximately one-third of your supply should be 400-speed film for dark, rainy days or evenings. Buying two different speeds of film means you should have at least one camera filled with each type so that you can get good pictures under most light conditions.

Endless numbers of photography books are available that offer tips on how to shoot good pictures, so we will not attempt to do that here. But we will offer you our own advice on taking photographs while camping with kids:

•Try to include people, especially family members or friends, in every photograph. People lend perspective to a picture, particularly one of a scenic setting, as well as helping illustrate the story of your family's trip.

•Candid pictures of family members enjoying themselves while canoeing, horseback riding, panning for gold or engaged in some other activity are an excellent way to illustrate the trip, but a candid picture of the back of a person's head is boring. Often, a posed picture is better than a candid one, even if the subject is smiling at the camera.

•Don't neglect to take pictures of even the routine camping activities -- cleaning fish, cooking over a campfire, hiking in the woods, etc.

•Try to shoot every photograph from three positions -- a long-distance one, a medium-range one and a close-up. You will be surprised at the different perspective you will get for basically the same picture.

•When possible, shoot scenic pictures in the early morning or late afternoon when the sun is lowest, creating long shadows and warm colors.

•Be aware of ugly intrusions when trying to shoot scenery. Telephone lines and power poles can turn a beautiful scene into an ordinary photograph.

•No matter what you do, you probably will not create photos that will do justice to a panoramic setting such as the Grand Canyon or a mountain. Shoot pictures of family members instead, with the panorama used as a backdrop. Buy your panoramic slides or photographs from a nearby gift shop.

•Shooting pictures across a lake or stream is a waste of film. A flat body of water is not scenic when reduced to snapshot size. Again, put a person in the foreground for perspective.

•Try shooting pictures with the camera off its automatic setting and positioned on various exposures and speeds. You'll be surprised by the results, and you might even produce some really remarkable photos.

•After you have experimented with camera exposures and speeds, "bracket" your shots using various speed/exposure combinations in order to produce a wider variety of picture brightness and darkness. Once you become accustomed to bracketing your shots, you'll discover that you are enjoying the photography more and are getting better results than the automatic setting can provide.

Chapter 17

Wild Animals

As we all know, suburbia has encroached upon the natural habitat of wild animals all over the world, forcing those animals either to migrate elsewhere or adjust to the presence of man. Most of us have not considered, however, that a more direct invasion of animal habitats takes place every time we go camping. When we trek into a wilderness in our RV or with our tents, we are taking a portion of our society with us into a foreign environment that has no need for it.

When we do that, we should remember that we are the interlopers, not the wild animals that come calling at night, searching for food in our trash cans or even in our sleeping bags. Wild animals must carry out a never-ending search for food, and they are unaware of any rules of nature which state they cannot hunt for it in our camp. After all, when we take a huge supply of groceries into the wilderness, we are in effect inviting the creatures of the forest to share our bounty with us.

Like the wild animals that have learned to cope with encroaching suburbia, wilderness animals also have learned to live with camping families.

We won't deal with how you ought to protect your supplies and equipment from those animals (there are several books available on that subject). Since our discussion focuses on camping with kids, we want to emphasize a few points about taking your children camping in areas where wild animals are present.

First, recognize that one of the lessons wild animals learn very quickly about campers is that most camping families will feed them. That means all they have to do is make their presence felt, and they will be rewarded with handouts. Raccoons, skunks, bears, squirrels, wild burros and a variety of other animals quickly become adept at begging food from campers. Another lesson the animals learn

quickly is that campers leave a lot of food and supplies ly-
ing around untended. And, they learn, when the campers
are sleeping or gone from the campsite, those items are
easy pickings.

Combine these two lessons, and the campers are faced with an unpleasant set of circumstances. If they feed
the animals, the animals will make a nuisance of themselves and eat everything that can be tossed to them. Then
if the feeding stops, the animals will invade the campsite
looking for food themselves. In fact, that invasion probably
will take place whether or not the campers provide handouts!

DON'T FEED THE ANIMALS

Our advice is to accept that fact, protect your food
and supplies the best you can and ignore the wild animals
that wander around your site at night. Under no circumstances should you feed them!

Much more importantly, however, you should never,
never try to touch a wild animal! Cute as they are, they are
not pets; they are wild predators, and they neither want nor
need your affection. Countless children have been seriously
bitten by cute animals that were searching for food, not affection.

Animal bites can be painful and, in some cases, even
life-threatening. The biggest danger to children and pets is
from rabid animals. Raccoons, squirrels and several other
species of animals can carry rabies, but by far the highest
incidence of rabies is with skunks. Research has shown that
the proportion of skunks carrying rabies often is more than
30%. City-bred children and pets that are taken into the
wilderness unprepared can be in real danger from those a
animals.

Make sure your pets are inoculated against rabies before taking them on a camping trip, and educate your children about the potential dangers from wild animals. We recommend setting a strict rule that no one is to pet or feed animals. They are quite capable of finding food that is better suited to their digestive systems than any table scraps you can give them.

Certainly, wild animals are beautiful. It is a rare pleasure to watch them in their natural environment as you camp. We encourage you to watch them all you wish, and even photograph them. Take a hike early in the morning and look for animal tracks in the dirt or sand. Make a camping project out of listing the various kinds of animals or animal tracks that are observed. Live with the animals, share the forest with them, but don't try to make pets out of them.

Chapter 18

Fishing With Kids

Fishing is the number one activity of American campers. It also is an excellent pasttime for kids because the destinations of most parents who take their kids camping are campsites near ponds, lakes or streams. Kids enjoy fishing even when their parents do not, but if either of the parents is a fisherman too, a camping trip that includes fishing can become even more enjoyable for the youngsters.

We started fishing with our children when they were old enough to hold a pole with line tied to the end of it. We'll never forget the time we took Sarah out in our boat fishing when she was about two years old. We provided her with a short ice-fishing rod about two feet long, and we rigged it with a line, a hook and a bobber. By dropping the bait over the side of the boat, and watching the worm through the clear water, Sarah was able to see the fish feed. She had a great time catching fish for about an hour. She hauled them in and held them to her chest while she re-

Simple, easy-to-use gear is best for beginners...

Don't insist that kids touch the fish or bait their own hooks...

moved the hooks, but then she announced, "I'm tired!" and she dropped her new rod overboard into the water.

We had forgotten an important rule about fishing with kids: They have a very short attention span.

Keep that in mind as you plan a fishing outing with your kids. The older they are, of course, the longer they can fish, and once they become veteran anglers, they will outfish their parents in terms of time spent on the water. Two of our three sons and our only daughter enjoy fishing very much; our other son, Thad, would rather do almost anything else. Don, who also learned to fish as a child, now has three confirmed fishing buddies. And quite often while they're fishing on a lake somewhere, Pam and Thad go shopping or sightseeing together.

When starting to fish with kids, equip them with the simplest gear possible, keeping in mind their age and physical capabilities. Very small children need only a pole, line, hook, bobber and live bait or small lure. Once a child is about five years old, though, he expects to have his own rod, reel, lures and tacklebox. Beginners' spincast reels, with rods and line, can be purchased at most discount stores for under $15, and sometimes for under $10. We don't recommend purchasing a cheap, all-plastic reel made by an off-brand manufacturer, however. Buy a Zebco outfit or one made by an equally well known company. It will be less likely to jam or fall apart in the middle of a fishing outing.

Small lures such as jigs, plastic grubs and spinners -- all sized for panfish (bluegills and crappies) -- are excellent baits for children to use. They will catch lots of fish most of the time, and occasionally, they will even attract the attention of a large game fish. Live bait such as worms, nightcrawlers, crickets and minnows will consistently catch

If a young fisherman asks to unhook his fish, let him...

more fish, but they are more difficult to handle and keep alive.

Do not insist that a child unhook his fish. Don made that mistake with Thad, and it is one of the reasons Thad did not enjoy fishing. We learned from that mistake, however, and when Sarah and Micah started fishing, we unhooked the fish for them and showed them how it was done. After watching us do it a few times, they begged to do it themselves! Although we believe the kids should be encouraged to tie on their own lures after being shown how to tie appropriate knots, we also don't recommend forcing a child to bait his own hook with live bait. Ask them to try it, but if they don't like baiting their hooks, do it for them.

ACTIVE OR LAID-BACK FISHING

Ideally, a fishing outing will include using both live bait and artificial lures. That way, the child can actively stalk fish by casting and retrieving the lures, or he can fish in a more relaxed way by watching the bobber. Once, we took our kids fishing in a boat on a clear, secluded lake in Canada. We had no idea what kind of fish were in the lake before we launched the boat, but we quickly found a huge school of small sunfish. The fish swarmed under our boat, and all the kids had to do to catch them was to drop a small artificial lure over the side and move it up and down a couple of times. They caught hundreds of fish (all of which we returned to the water) in a very short time and enjoyed themselves immensely.

To provide your kids with lots of fishing action, look for bluegills around a dock or pier, where the bank drops steeply into the water, and where there are large rocks or other underwater cover. Fish as close to the bottom as possible.

While our kids were quite young, we started teaching them good conservation habits. We never kept undersized fish, and we allowed the kids to return their catches to the water themselves if they wished to do so. Even if a large fish were caught, we put it back if we did not intend to eat it immediately or if we did not catch enough for a meal. Sometimes, that practice backfired. Once, fishing in Tennessee, nine-year-old Chris caught a trophy-size largemouth bass, and Don convinced him to return it to the water. Chris wanted to keep that fish, even though he accepted the reasons for releasing it. Now, nearly 20 years later, Chris occasionally mentions the time his Dad made him throw back the biggest fish he ever caught!

Because our family likes fishing so much, traveling and camping in a motorhome is ideal for us because we can tow our bassboat behind us and never be concerned about whether we can find a boat to rent. When we go on a family camping vacation, we also enjoy searching out secluded, off-the-beaten-track lakes where we can launch our boat and enjoy fishing without seeing or hearing any other people. With a little practice, a boat can be launched quite easily with a motorhome, even a coach 35 feet long!

Traveling in motorhomes and towing our boat, we have camped and fished throughout the country, and our kids have caught fish from bodies of water that their non-camping friends only read about in the outdoor magazines.

Chapter 19

Safety and First-Aid

Two of our best friends are Hal and Penny Gaynor, a 70-year-old couple that retired 20 years ago and almost immediately began living and traveling in an RV full time. During those two decades they built a national reputation among campers for the free camping safety seminars they hold at campgrounds, RV club rallies and travel/vacation shows. They operate the widely respected and much-in-demand RV Safety Clinic. In their safety seminars, they offer tips on how families can go camping more safely, and there is no question in our minds that they have saved lives by emphasizing safety. The seminars are a combination of serious advice and humorous stories, and although we have attended their sessions several times, we laugh whenever we hear their stories and jokes, and we learn more about camping each time they offer their safety tips.

Hal and Penny's motto is "Safety is Fun." When we first met them about 15 years ago, we thought that was a silly motto. Safety, we thought, was desirable, but DULL!

Now that we've raised four children in the camping life-style, we have a clearer interpretation of their motto's meaning. Maybe practicing safety is not exactly fun, but camping is fun, and safe camping with kids ensures that the whole family will enjoy camping to the fullest extent possible.

Hal and Penny don't just preach safety, they practice it too. They turn off their RV's LP-gas tank before doing any traveling. They do not use their LP-fueled appliances while on the road. They always check the polarity of a campground's electrical system before settling into a site. They do not do anything that is even remotely unsafe. And in spite of their living habits and expertise, their travel trailer once caught on fire and burned to the ground along with everything in it.

If it can happen to them, it can happen to us. Or to you.

TEACH KIDS ABOUT SAFETY

Practicing safety while camping with kids is essential. Our kids are too precious for us not to consider their welfare and safety at all times. So although we do not live safety the way Hal and Penny do, we try to practice it, and we taught our children to practice it too.

Many aspects of safe camping with kids involve using common sense and extending home-safety concepts into a campsite setting. For example, at home we routinely place sharp or dangerous objects out of the reach of small children; we should do that in the campground too. Hot camp stoves, knives, fishing hooks and lures, matches, camp tools and similar items should be placed where small hands cannot reach them. And just as small children are prevented from burning themselves on a cooking range at home, so too should they be kept away from campfires and barbecue pits, where even the flameless coals could be hot.

As every parent knows, there are good reasons for all members of the family to be immunized regularly against tetanus (every ten years for adults, every five years for children). Camping in an outdoor environment adds even more emphasis to the need for tetanus shots, especially for children.

INSTRUCTIONS AND PRACTICES

During a typical vacation with kids, there are two primary aspects of safe camping: safety instructions and safe practices. Safety instructions include teaching the kids about fire extinguishers, where they are and how to use them; how to purify water for drinking; how to use a first-aid kit, how to exit a tent or RV in case of a fire or other emergency; how to detect and stop LP-gas leaks; what to do in case a person's clothes catch on fire; what a smoke alarm sounds like and what to do if it sounds; how to extinguish a campfire or a wood cooking fire; preventing forest fires; how to handle matches safely. Safety practices include avoiding fatigue while driving; shutting off LP-gas valves when traveling; avoiding low bridges or other obstructions with an RV; taking appropriate fire-prevention steps when refueling while towing a travel trailer or driving a motorhome; packing a camping vehicle so it is not overloaded; equipping a rig with the right safety tools; making safe turns with an RV; coping with high cross-winds while traveling.

THE RIGHT PRECAUTIONS

Hal and Penny Gaynor could have avoided their trailer fire if they had taken one precaution, but they did not know about it. Habitually, they put a nightlight -- exactly the same kind used in children's bedrooms! -- in the electrical outlet of their trailer's hallway. The bulb overheated its plastic cover, and a fire started that spread quickly up the wall and then throughout the coach. The Gaynors now tell other campers how they can avoid similar experiences, and they firmly believe all campers, and especially children, should be instructed about all aspects of camping safety.

FIRE EXTINGUISHERS

Fire safety experts strongly recommend that everyone in a family attend short classes on fire extinguishers held by many local fire departments. At those classes, hands-on instruction is given on how to operate various kinds of extinguishers and the proper ways to put out fires. Extinguishers are rated according to their effectiveness on different types of fires: Class A extinguishers are used for paper, wood, rubber, plastic and fabric fires; Class B, for flammable liquids such as propane, gasoline or paint; Class C, for electrical motors, switches and appliances.

The most common extinguisher carried by campers is a 2.5-pound Class ABC model which can be used for most types of fires. Some persons carry Class AB extinguishers, but we do not recommend those because they are not suitable for electrical fires. In our offices, we keep a 2.5-pound Class ABC Halon extinguisher purchased for us by Hal and Penny Gaynor; it is an excellent model for tent or RV-camping. When camped, keep the extinguisher near the galley.

WATER PURIFICATION

When we were children, safe drinking water could be found almost anywhere, including in springs, wells and remote wilderness lakes. Today, campers must regard all such water as polluted and contaminated with a bacteria called giardia that is transmitted by animal and human waste.

If lake or stream water is the only water available for drinking, however, it can be purified by boiling or by using commercial water purification tablets (available at most camping supplies stores). We recommend boiling most water for 30 minutes, and 50 per cent longer than that if you are camping at an altitude of 5,000 to 8,000 feet.

FIRST-AID KITS

A home-style first-aid kit can be quite useful when camping with kids, but it probably will have to be expanded in order to fit a family's outdoor living needs. We do recommend that families pack a copy of their home medical book if possible because most of those books are quite helpful when parents try to analyze the symptoms and treatments of swellings, punctures, burns, scrapes and illnesses. Excellent kits can be purchased, but chances are their contents will have to be modified to include more items. Here are our suggested contents for a family's camping first-aid kit:

- Adhesive bandages in various sizes
- Ace bandages
- Alcohol
- Antacid tablets
- Adhesive tape
- Antibiotic ointment
- Antiseptic soap

- Antiseptic spray
- Bee sting ointment
- Constipation medicine
- Cotton balls
- Diarrhea medicine
- Gauze rolls
- Insect repellent
- Lip balm
- Moist towelettes
- Safety pins
- Scissors
- Thermometer
- Tweezers
- Aspirin
- Calamine lotion
- Cortisone cream
- Cotton swabs
- Gauze pads
- Hydrogen peroxide
- Ipecac syrup
- Medicated powder
- Needles
- Salt tablets
- Sunscreen
- Throat lozenges
- Water purification tablets

FIRE DRILLS

Guiltily, we have to admit that although we often talked with our kids about what to do in case of a tent or RV fire, we never actually held any fire drills, although we intended to do it. Whether you schedule drills or not, you should make certain the kids know about their exit options. In a tent, there are two choices if the front of the tent is blocked by flames: Either jerk the stakes out of the ground at the rear of the tent or use a sharp knife to cut a hole in the rear wall. Every RV has at least two primary exits -- the entry door and a designated emergency exit (nearly always a window) that is required by law. Other windows on an RV also can be exited in an emergency. Large slider windows can simply be opened and the screens either opened or pushed out. The glass in some types of windows must be smashed, but depending upon how the windows are mounted, that may not be very difficult. In some motorhomes, windshields can be kicked out from the inside rather easily.

Fire drills should include grabbing the fire extinguishers if they are within easy reach, but no one should attempt to save any possessions. If it is convenient to do so, shut off an RV's LP lines at the tanks; if that cannot be done safely, do not attempt it. Once outside, retreat some distance from the RV or tent in case the fire results in explosions, and immediately call the local fire department from the nearest phone or ask someone else to make the call for you. Never try going back inside a burning structure.

STOP, DROP AND ROLL

If any family member's clothing catches fire at any time, everyone else should shout for him to go through the widely accepted drill of stop, drop and roll. Running with clothing afire only fans the flames, so the first requirement is to stop trying to run away from the fire. Then drop to the ground and roll on the flames to smother them. Other family members should help by using a coat or some other heavy covering material to help smother the flames; tent fabric or a tent ground cloth serves this function quite well.

DETECTING LP-GAS LEAKS

Hal and Penny Gaynor frequently tell campers that husbands should always believe their wives when the wives claim they smell LP-gas. "A woman's nose knows," Penny says emphatically. LP-gas is odorless, but a rotten-egg scent is added to assist in leak detection. LP-gas also is heavier than air and falls to the lowest level it can reach and collects there. Don't ever try to find an LP leak by striking a match; that can easily spark an explosion or fire. Instead, apply soapy water to joints in the gas line, beginning with the connections at the appliance where the leak is suspected.

LP-gas leak detectors which shut off the gas flow as soon as they detect a leak are available from camping supply stores. We recommend that every RV have one.

AVOIDING FATIGUE WHILE DRIVING

Remember those camping trips we talked about starting in the middle of the night? It was not very smart of us to do that, but no one could have convinced us, so we won't try to convince you not to do it either. Every travel expert we've been exposed to recommends not driving more than 300 miles during a 24-hour period. That means six to eight hours of battling traffic and fatigue. Experts also suggest stopping every two or three hours to change drivers or walk around. Night driving should be avoided, according to the same experts. It all sounds like good advice to us.

SHUT OFF LP-GAS VALVES

As we mentioned earlier, camping safety experts Hal and Penny Gaynor always shut off their RV's LP-gas valves before they leave a campground in the morning for travel to their next destination. They strongly urge other

RVers to do the same thing. The reason is simple: Constant highway movement and shifting of the RV structure can result in loose or broken LP lines. They also refuse to travel with the LP-fueled appliances on, even the refrigerator, because they claim evidence shows the small flame on the refrigerator can produce a devastating RV fire if the gas lines break or spring a leak. As part of their safety seminars, they explain how RVers can travel without operating their refrigerators and still not risk food spoilage. Catch one of their seminars so you can hear their explanation for yourself.

REFUELING AN RV

Hal Gaynor is able to document other experts' long-standing claim that if LP-fueled RV appliances are not turned off during refueling stops at gasoline service stations, an explosion or fire can result. Federal laws require RV appliances to be turned off during refueling stops, but most RVers do not do it. The small pilot flames of the appliances have, on several occasions, caused fires by igniting gasoline fumes escaping from the service station's pumps. Hal believes so strongly in the danger from lighted RV appliances that he refuses to refuel at any service station where another RV is already stopped!

AVOIDING LOW BRIDGES

Trying to tow a 12-foot-tall trailer under a 10-foot-high overpass can have disastrous results, as anyone who has crunched the front end of an RV that way can testify.

For the safety of your family as well as to prevent damage
to your RV, measure your coach from the road to its tallest
point (usually the top of an air conditioner) and then post
that height in front of your camping vehicle's driver where
it cannot be forgotten. Interstate highways and designated
U.S. routes will not offer you low-clearance obstructions
such as bridges and overpasses, but the same cannot be said
for secondary roads and state highways. We have also
heard of examples where interstate highway traffic has been
detoured onto roads with low clearances, resulting in a sud-
den rash of truck and RV-crunching.

SAFETY GEAR

Special tools and equipment ordinarily is not required
when going on a family camping trip, but there are occasions when such items might be desirable. When driving
through a large unpopulated area or a spacious wilderness
like Alaska or sections of Canada, safety equipment could
transform a potential highway disaster into a minor inconvenience. Gear such as a flashlight, first-aid kit, fire extinguisher, sleeping bags, hand tools, jumper cables, spare
fuses, a jack and lug wrench probably are already packed
into the camping vehicles, especially if you've followed our
packing recommendations.

Other desirable gear that you probably would not
take on a routine camping trip include tow chain or strap,
tire gauge and pump, tire chains, flares and a shovel.

TREATING INJURIES

Every member of a camping family who could possibly be

in the responsible position of treating the minor injuries of another family member should learn how to perform those duties prior to leaving on the trip. We recommend either enrolling in a Red Cross first-aid course or reading some of the many books on first-aid treatment of cuts, burns, blisters, bee stings, insect bites, poison ivy and tick bites. And while you're at it, learn the best ways for removing a fish hook from small fingers and hands!

Chapter 20

Water Conservation

Many parts of our country are experiencing water shortages of such a magnitude that dramatic rationing and conservation measures are being taken. Water conservation is an issue that has long been a familiar one to camping families, however. Water conservation is an inherent part of the camping lifestyle, not because water is in short supply, but because campers often do not have immediate access to it.

We have believed for several years that a significant proportion of our country's water supply problems could be solved if households would only practice the kind of conservation that is routine with campers. In fact, on the rare occasions that our home septic system has had drainage difficulties, we have told our kids, "Take RV showers." They know that means they must run only enough water to wet their bodies, soap down and rinse off; they cannot allow the shower to operate while they are doing that. The "RV shower" routine provides enough water to wash, but not enough for an orgy of soaking. Typically, one of those showers uses less than three gallons of water compared with ten times that amount for a leisurely 10-minute bath-time experience.

While RV camping, we also use minimal amounts of water for flushing the toilet, brushing teeth and washing dishes. Faucets are never permitted to produce more than just enough water to do the job. RV-camping without city water hookup means that only the water carried in the coach's 20-40 gallon storage tank is available for use, and if there are no sewage emptying systems available, any water that is wasted can also fill the RV's holding tanks quickly.

HARDER FOR TENT-CAMPERS

Tent-campers often face even more pressure for water conservation than RV-campers, especially when they must carry water to their site by hand after collecting it from a spring or stream or pumping it from a well. families that camp away from developed campgrounds frequently have only the cooking and drinking water that can be carried in a jug; they must depend upon streams, waterfalls, lakes or portable cold-water showers for bathing.

Because water conservation is such an important part of camping life, children should be taught conserving routines at the earliest possible opportunity. We recommend practicing the routines even when using campground bath facilities. Do not take the position that when you pay your campsite fee, you are paying for all the water you want to use. Water is, after all, a natural resource that must be preserved for future generations because it is not replenishing itself in many parts of the country as quickly as it is being used.

Taught conservation practices at an early age, camping kids are likely to continue those practices into adulthood and pass them on to their own children.

Chapter 21

Rainy Day Blues

Parents who plan to take their kids camping for the first time worry too much about how they will keep the kids occupied if bad weather prevents the children from being outdoors. Rainy-day boredom is a problem at home, so it certainly must be a worse problem when camping, they reason.

Not true. Rainy days can present a camping family with excellent opportunities to broaden their experiences. In fact, when we take a camping vacation, we build into our schedule several contingency plans that include exploring, sightseeing, shopping and visiting interesting attractions. If poor weather persists for several days, we are able to fall back on camp-based activities and games, but doing that has seldom been necessary.

Like most other campers, we are always in search of new adventures and new places to go camping. So for us, a rainy day that discourages our usual camp activities simply encourages us to leave camp and explore. To prepare for that kind of outing, before we leave home we write to various local tourism bureaus and chambers of commerce for information about their highlights. Typically, we will select two or three potential areas that we think we might like to visit for a future vacation, and we will check out those places on rainy days.

If we like the first area we visit, we might not even go to the others but instead, spend the day talking with people and looking over campgrounds, shopping areas, attractions and recreational opportunities. We collect all the brochures and literature we can, pointedly stopping at a local tourist bureau, information center or chamber of commerce if the area has one. State and national parks and forests that provide camping spaces are considered as well as privately developed campgrounds. Because fishing is one of our family's favorite activities, we will find out what kinds of fish are caught in the area and at least drive past a couple of the lakes or streams that sound interesting to us.

Because we write books and magazine articles on travel and camping, we probably will do a little research on the area's appeal to tourists in case we think we'd like to write about it in the future. We especially look for free or low-cost campsites and free attractions that we can include in the updates to our books on those topics.

While we are exploring the area, however, we always try to keep in mind that our kids are not at all interested in most of the information-gathering that we are doing. They want fun and activities. So for their benefit, as well as for background writing research, we will try to find a couple of family-type attractions -- an amusement park, a cavern tour, a museum, a wildlife sanctuary, a fish hatchery, a water park. If we did a good job in our pre-trip planning, we should have a wealth of tourist information at

Authors' family visits Indianapolis Speedway Museum...

our fingertips that we collected before leaving home, and that information should tell us about the best attractions in the area.

It has been our experience, however, that every area has attractions or interesting features which are not widely publicized in tourist literature. We enjoy discovering those for ourselves and, for that reason, frequently make a point of asking local residents what they like to do and where they like to go for entertainment. Fish hatcheries and museums that focus on local history are two such attractions. During one vacation, we spent half a day visiting a small museum south of Red Wing, Minnesota, that was filled with fascinating artifacts from the era when paddleboats and steamboats traveled the upper Mississippi River which was only a stone's throw away. On another trip to the Pacific Northwest, we stopped at a dam and fish hatchery in Oregon where we watched hundreds of beautiful salmon swim upstream to spawn and we learned about the state's efforts to preserve its threatened salmon fishery.

At times, we have been so intrigued by the new area we are visiting that we've decided to spend the rest of our vacation there instead of waiting for another trip to do it. The freedom to break camp and travel on an impulse is one of the most important features to us about camping, and it is the primary reason we refuse to commit to long-term camping at one site unless absolutely necessary.

If your family feels more secure spending its rainy days in camp together, there are still dozens of activities that can keep children quietly occupied until the weather improves.

The pine cones, shells or beach treasures found earlier can be made into Christmas tree decorations. A rain gauge can be made by marking one-inch and half-inch measurements on the outside of a tall, narrow olive jar with a felt-tipped marker; set a larger wide-mouthed container outside in the rain to collect water, and every hour, pour the rainwater from the large container into the olive jar to measure the amount of rainfall. Hold a family discussion about weather, covering topics such as clouds, lightning, thunder and rainbows. Parents could encourage small children to illustrate the rainy day by drawing pictures of the campground, complete with a thunderstorm, lightning and a rainbow. Rocks that were collected earlier can be polished while the rain falls; leaf collections can be pressed and identified.

Rainy days can be spent reading books, playing cards or board games, telling ghost stories or even just napping. It's a good time for quiet, lazy activities and relaxing. But then, that is part of the reason for taking a vacation!

Chapter 22

Keeping a Travel Log

Our kids started keeping travel logs and vacation diaries when they were young simply because they were not happy with the way their Mom maintained hers! They thought she did not include enough information in it. If we visited an attraction while we were traveling, they wanted a record made of where the attraction was, how much its entry fees were, what it contained, what their thoughts were about it and whether they liked it enough to return in the future. They also wanted to record details of everything they did each day: when they awoke, what they ate for each meal, what they did, what kinds of lures they used to catch fish, how big the fish were and exactly where they were caught, the names and addresses of new friends met that day and what their plans were for the next day.

For her part, Pam was content to keep track of fuel, food and gasoline costs along with the number of miles traveled on each tank of gasoline.

The kids thought she was missing the whole point of

keeping a travel log!

In retrospect, the kids were probably right. From time to time, we have reviewed one of the kids' travel logs, and the notations about their camping experiences gave us a broader appreciation of the experiences we enjoyed as we traveled and camped together. The entries about our expenses turned out to be less important to us than we expected. Today, we don't really care how much we spent on our caravan trip to Boise, Idaho; but we enjoy recalling and reliving all the wonderful things we did with each other and with the friends who traveled in our caravans. That trip, as well as so many others that we remember now, was a once-in-a-lifetime experience that can never be duplicated. The kids' travel logs help remind us of that.

ONE FOR EACH CHILD

We strongly recommend that each child old enough to write be provided with a personal travel diary for every trip. A diary meant to contain several trips is not as appealing, although we think children might find an annual diary to be worthwhile. By keeping a diary of each vacation, or each year's trips, the child can create his own travel library, marking individual log books with the year entries were made.

A travel log that can be used both by adults and children should contain enough blank (preferably lined) pages for at least 22 days (and preferably 30 days) of private diary-type memory entries. It should include time-and-distance charts for noting departure and arrival times along with miles traveled. Charts that provide easy calculations of fuel economy also are necessary. Another valuable chart is one that enables shopping expenses to be recorded: the date, the type of items purchased, the name and location of the store where the purchase was made, and the cost. Logs of photographs are quite valuable for children; the type welike best provides easy entries of a film roll's number, its ASA and then identification of each frame on a 36-exposure roll, including subject photographed, F-stop setting, speed setting and location. Ideally, a log should have a section for names, addresses and phone numbers of new friends, along with space for notations about them.

Several commercially produced log books contain some or most of these features, but in our experience nearly all those books are either produced in poor formats or they are too expensive. Greedy log-book publishers quite often try to build in repeat business for themselves by producing loose-leaf or plastic-ring bound books for which new fillers must be purchased. We would much rather use a professionally printed book that is "perfect-bound" like the book you are reading.

SIZE AND PRICE IMPORTANT

Also, log books tend to be sized without much consideration given to how they will be used. Therefore, they nearly always are too large to be stored easily or they are too small to encourage legible entries. Because we believe a new log book should be used for every camping trip, or at most for a year of trips, its price should reflect that kind of usage and be low enough to encourage children to build their own log book libraries. Log book prices of $10-14 are quite high, but marginally acceptable, while those costing $18-25 are unreasonably expensive. A price in the $7-10 range is more appropriate.

Over the years, we have examined and used a wide variety of travel diaries, but until recently we did not find one that fit all the requirements we have outlined here. The

Career Press, a New Jersey-based book publisher and distributor, asked us to examine the format of a diary it was considering publishing, and we offered suggestions for changes to include the requirements we believe camping families need. To our surprise, the company accepted our recommendations and produced what we consider to be the best book of its kind available.

Titled *My RV/Camping Travel Planner and Trip Diary*, it is in a handy, six-inch by nine-inch perfect-bound format that fits easily under a car seat, on the dashboard or in the glove compartment. Not only does it contain all the necessary features, but it also has special sections of its own that other travel logs do not offer.

CHARTS AND CHECKLISTS

For example, in the front is an annual planning chart that provides space for 31 days of entries each month of the year -- a useful feature that never occurred to us. Along with that chart are three blank, block-format monthly calendar pages that can be custom-prepared for 90 days of travel planning. Those pages are followed by detailed checklists for trip preparations, auto and RV maintenance, camping equipment, supplies and food. A page provides space for important information that you might need while traveling: credit card and traveler's check numbers and the names and phone numbers of your family doctor, dentist, pharmacy, attorney, bank and travel club.

A travel reference section provides a list of state tourist information centers and their toll-free telephone numbers, a highway mileage chart of major U.S. cities, month-by-month information on the number of sunny days and average temperatures in each state, a state-by-state list of highway restrictions for automobiles and RVs, and the toll-free phone numbers of more than 50 hotel and motel chains.

Best of all, this useful new log book is priced at only $6.95! That is about half the cost of competitive travel diaries that do not contain the right kinds of charts, forms and information. Copies are available in bookstores, some retail outlets that sell camping supplies, or from the publisher, Career Press, P.O. Box 34, Hawthorne, NJ 07507; phone 1-800/227-3371.

Chapter 23

"We'll stop there on the way back!"

We hope you are ready to start planning a camping trip with your kids. We've tried to provide you with tips based on the full range of our experience and observations while camping with our own children, and we hope you find those tips useful. You'll probably follow some of our recomendations and decide that others do not apply to you. A few suggestions you will reject flatly for various reasons, only to decide at some period in the future that maybe we were right about them.

That's the way it goes. Camping is just a form of living, and living has to be practiced a day at a time and by the seat of our pants.

We can't leave you, though, without a final word about a common family traveling phenomenon. We'll offer it to you without advice or recommendations and ask only that you accept it as true.

During one of our family's early camping trips to Lake Cumberland in southern Kentucky, we drove through a small country town with a rustic (actually, it was dilapidated!) antique store on its southern edge. Out front was a huge black cast-iron kettle like the ones in which farm families used to do their laundry. Pam and our two oldest sons were excited by seeing it because they had shopped for a kettle like that for several months. They wanted to stop and buy it.

Don, always the practical traveler, pointed out how difficult it would be to haul that kettle to Lake Cumberland in our small mini-motorhome, unload it and load it at the campsite and camp around it while we were there. He said, "We'll stop there and buy it on the way back home." That argument made sense, so the family agreed to it.

But plans change.

A NEW ROUTE BECKONS

Following our camping weekend at the lake, we traveled a different route part of the way home because, Don said, we had never gone that way before, and we ought to explore alternative routes whenever we could. Of course, the new route did not go near the little town with the antique store. But Don said, "We'll stop there the next time we're in the area."

Okay.

That was in the mid-1970s, nearly twenty years ago. Pam and the boys still have not been able to find a large black cast-iron kettle like the one that was for sale at that little town's antique store, and for various reasons, we never traveled through that town again during the times the antique store was open. We drove past the shop many times during the 1970s, and the kettle was still for sale each time, but there was no one at the store to sell it to us! And Don always said, "We'll stop there on the way back" or "We'll go there the next time we're in the area."

Now, it is 1992, and Pam and the boys still have not been able to find a huge black cast-iron kettle like the one that was in front of the antique store in that little Kentucky town.

During the intervening years, our family has camped virtually everywhere in north America except Alaska and the western Canadian provinces. From time to time, the kids have begged to stop at one location or another so that they could visit an attraction or buy a gift or renew an old friendship, and quite often they were told, "We'll stop there on the way back." We've enjoyed a lifetime of experiences traveling and camping with our kids. But we suspect we've also missed an equal number of experiences because it was not convenient for us to stop.

Our intentions are good, though. We'll go there the next time we're in the area.